A LANGUAGE GUIDE FOR BEGINNERS

Learning
Korean

Learn to Speak, Read and Write Korean Quickly!

JULIE DAMRON & JUNO BAIK

TUTTLE Publishing

Tokyo | Rutland, Vermont | Singapore

"Books to Span the East and West"

Tuttle Publishing was founded in 1832 in the small New England town of Rutland, Vermont [USA]. Our core values remain as strong today as they were then—to publish best-in-class books which bring people together one page at a time. In 1948, we established a publishing office in Japan—and Tuttle is now a leader in publishing English-language books about the arts, languages and cultures of Asia. The world has become a much smaller place today and Asia's economic and cultural influence has grown. Yet the need for meaningful dialogue and information about this diverse region has never been greater. Over the past seven decades, Tuttle has published thousands of books on subjects ranging from martial arts and paper crafts to language learning and literature—and our talented authors, illustrators, designers and photographers have won many prestigious awards. We welcome you to explore the wealth of information available on Asia at **www.tuttlepublishing.com**.

Published by Tuttle Publishing, an imprint of Periplus Editions (HK) Ltd.

www.tuttlepublishing.com

Copyright © 2022 by Julie Damron

Library of Congress Catalog-in-Publication Data in progress

ISBN 978-0-8048-5332-3

First edition, 2022

Distributed by

North America, Latin America & Europe
Tuttle Publishing
364 Innovation Drive
North Clarendon,
VT 05759-9436 U.S.A.
Tel: 1 (802) 773-8930
Fax: 1 (802) 773-6993
info@tuttlepublishing.com
www.tuttlepublishing.com

Japan
Tuttle Publishing
Yaekari Building, 3rd Floor,
5-4-12 Osaki, Shinagawa-ku,
Tokyo 141 0032
Tel: (81) 3 5437-017
Fax: (81) 3 5437-0755
sales@tuttle.co.jp
www.tuttle.co.jp

Asia Pacific
Berkeley Books Pte. Ltd.
3 Kallang Sector #04-01
Singapore 349278
Tel: (65) 6741-2178
Fax: (65) 6741-2179
inquiries@periplus.com.sg
www.tuttlepublishing.com

25 24 23 22   5 4 3 2 1

Printed in Malaysia   2202VP

TUTTLE PUBLISHING® is a registered trademark of Tuttle Publishing, a division of Periplus Editions (HK) Ltd.

Contents

Preface

Our purpose in writing this book is to fill a need among our Brigham Young University (BYU) students learning Korean and traveling to Korea for a semester of study abroad. With varying levels of Korean proficiency and in-country experience, they need a practical reference to help them with commonly-used expressions and vocabulary as well as information about cultural norms and expectations, instructions on how to use the transportation system, and information about popular sights and attractions they may want to visit. Although this book presents pertinent grammar and vocabulary, similar to a classroom textbook, its main purpose is to serve as a practical reference tool for people traveling to Korea for school, work or vacation.

I would like to thank my co-author, Professor Baik Juno as well as my BYU research assistant Park Soyoung and my students in the Korean 490r class who all contributed immensely to the content in these eleven chapters. I also want to thank our BYU student illustrator, Cydnee Gagnon.

Target Readership

Learning Korean is designed for beginning language learners who plan to travel, live or work in Korea. It not only teaches essential grammar, reading and writing, but provides commonly-used sentences and cultural etiquette so that foreigners in Korea can function successfully and appropriately.

How The Book Is Structured

Learning Korean is organized around the everyday situations you will encounter as a foreigner in Korea. Topics range from "Greetings and Essential Expressions" to "Dining Out." Each lesson, except the first one, contains three dialogues followed by explanations, vocabulary lists, grammar and cultural notes. The lessons are tailored to help you gain an understanding of Korea and the Korean language, so each lesson builds on the previous ones.

How to Use This Book

Dialogues: Learning how words and sentences are used in the spoken language is necessary for acquiring fluency. Each lesson has several dialogues, which demonstrate how the vocabulary and sentence structures in that lesson are actually used. They are useful for more advanced practice in later sections. They may also serve as outlines or templates, should you choose to expand upon them to create a more detailed conversation. We suggest that you listen to the audio recordings of each dialogue several times and memorize it before moving on to the next one.

Online Audio Recordings: Be sure to listen to the recordings for each dialogue before or as you read them, and try to memorize the dialogue. Doing so will help your pronunciation. Sometimes, you can listen to the entire recording and follow along, reading silently. Other times stop the audio at the end of each sentence and repeat what you have heard.

Lesson Vocabulary: Each section introduces and utilizes a new set of vocabulary. These words and sentences are compiled into Lesson Vocabulary lists, and are also available as printable flashcards (https://www.tuttlepublishing.com/learning-korean). Each section's vocabulary builds on those before it, so it is wise to memorize the vocabulary from each section before moving on to the next one.

Practice Activities: Each Dialogue has a variety of practice activities. If the activity has an audio component, the recommended procedure for using these is as follows:

1. Listen to the exchanges and think about the changes to make in response to the cues. Look back at the dialogues for examples if you are not sure what to do.
2. Listen to the first cue, insert your response during the pause, listen to the model answer, and repeat the model answer during the second pause.
3. Repeat this procedure for the following cues. It is recommended that you loop back to the beginning of the drill and run through it several times. Always try to respond to the cues before you listen to the model answer. Be sure you understand the meaning of what you are saying, and are not merely repeating the sounds.

Cultural Notes: In each lesson there will be a section titled *Cultural Notes.* These prepare you to explore Korean culture through the language, clarifying culturally important points and explaining the context in which certain language elements are appropriate.

Introduction to the Korean Language

The Korean language is one of the most widely spoken in the world, with over 77 million native speakers. Korean is spoken not only in Korea but in overseas Korean communities around the world. There are 8 million Korean heritage speakers in North America, China, Japan, the former Soviet Union and the European Union. With Korea's growing globalized economy and popular culture, learning Korean is becoming not only desirable but extremely valuable.

The Korean alphabet and writing system were designed to be simple, so learning to read and write Korean is fairly easy. As you read the following information about the Korean alphabet, syllables and sound changes, you will gain a better understanding of the language and how easy it is to read and write in Korean. We have provided romanized versions of the Korean words and sentences for easy reference, but we strongly recommend that you make the effort to learn the Korean Hangeul script.

The Pronunciation of Korean and the Hangeul Script

The Korean language has 21 basic vowel sounds and 19 basic consonant sounds. In the table below, the vowels and consonants are listed next to an English word that has a similar sound. Try reading them aloud to help your pronunciation and listen to the audio recordings of each sound.

1. Korean Vowels 🎧

Letter	English equivalent	Korean examples
ㅏ a	as in "father"	아버지 **abeoji** father
ㅓ eo	as in "sun"	어른 **eoreun** adult
ㅗ o	as in "home"	오늘 **oneul** today
ㅜ u	as in "lute"	우리 **uri** we
ㅡ eu	as in "book"	그림 **geurim** picture
ㅣ i	as in "police"	시간 **sigan** time
ㅐ ae	as in "sand"	개미 **gaemi** ant
ㅔ e	as in "pet"	에어컨 **eeokeon** aircondition
ㅚ oe	as in "wet"	쇠 **soe** steel
ㅟ wi	as in "we"	귀 **gwi** ear
ㅢ ui	combination of "book" + "police"	

Letter		English equivalent	Korean examples
ㅑ	ya	as in "yacht"	야구 yagu baseball
ㅕ	yeo	as in "young"	여자 yeoja woman
ㅛ	yo	as in "yo-yo"	요정 yojeong fairy
ㅠ	yu	as in "you/U"	유명 yumyeong famous
ㅐ	yae	as in "yank"	얘 yae hey
ㅖ	ye	as in "yet"	예절 yaejeol manners
ㅘ	wa	as in "watt"	과일 gwail fruits
ㅝ	wo	as in "won"	원자 wonja atom
ㅙ	wae	as in "way"	돼지 dwaeji pig
ㅞ	we	as in "west"	궤도 gwedo orbit

* **Note:** 애/-에, 얘/-예, 외/-왜, and 왜/-웨 were originally distinctive sounds, but in modern Korean, they sound the same.

2. Korean Consonants 🎧

Letter		English equivalent	Korean examples
ㄱ	g	as in "gum"	그네 geune swing
ㅋ	k	as in "khaki"	코 ko nose
ㄷ	d	as in "dime"	다락(방) darak(ppang) attic
ㅌ	t	as in "toe"	튀김 twigim fried food
ㅂ	b	as in "boat"	발코니 balkoni balcony
ㅍ	p	as in "pick"	포도 podo grape
ㅅ	s	as in "spoon" (aspirated)	사 sa four
ㅈ	j	as in "jam"	주말 jumal weekend
ㅎ	h	as in "happy"	하루 haru day
ㄴ	n	as in "noon"	나라 nara nation
ㅁ	m	as in "mom"	모자 moja hat
ㅇ	ng	as in "song"	농장 nongjang farm
ㄹ	l/r	as in "pal"/"run"	라면 ramyeon ramen
ㄲ	kk	as in "skewer"	까마귀 kkamagwi crow
ㄸ	tt	as in "stuck"	땀 ddam sweat
ㅃ	pp	as in "speak"	빵 bbang bread
ㅆ	ss	as in "sound"	썰매 sseolmae sled

Letter	English equivalent	Korean examples
ㅉ jj	as in "hats" (aspirated)	찌개 **jjigae** stew
ㅊ ch	as in "itch"	춤 **chum** dance

Learning the Korean Alphabet

The Korean alphabet is called Hangeul (한글). It is composed of 14 consonants and 10 vowels. As shown in the previous pages some consonants and vowels can be doubled or combined to form additional sounds.

1. Writing the Vowels 🎧

Practice writing the vowels and saying them out loud as you write them.

ㅑ ya						
ㅕ yeo						
ㅛ yo						
ㅠ yu						
ㅒ yae						
ㅖ ye						
ㅘ wa						
ㅝ wo						
ㅙ wae						
ㅞ we						

2. Writing the Consonants 🎧

Practice writing the consonants and pronouncing them out loud as you write them.

ㄱ g						
ㄴ n						
ㄷ d						
ㄹ l/r						

ㅁ m								
ㅂ b								
ㅅ s								
ㅇ ng								
ㅈ j								
ㅊ ch'								
ㅋ k'								
ㅌ t'								
ㅍ p'								
ㅎ h								
ㄲ kk								
ㄸ tt								
ㅃ pp								
ㅆ ss								
ㅉ jj								

* Note: "ㅇ" has no actual sound when it appears before any letter, but it has an **ng** sound when it is the last consonant in a syllable.

3. Writing Korean Syllables and Words

Korean words may look like thousands of different characters, but just as in English, they are actually formed by combining the letters of the alphabet to form syllables and words. The difference is that rather than being written horizontally on the same line, Korean letters are arranged in clusters.

In the following example, the Korean word 김치 (**kimchi**) is displayed in two clusters or syllables. The word 김치 **kimchi** is not two characters. Instead, it is one word made up of two syllables. The first syllable has three letters (ㄱ **k** + ㅣ **i** + ㅁ **m**) and the second syllable has two (ㅊ **ch** + ㅣ **i**). These are written as follows:

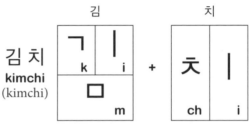

Whereas English syllables are written from left to right on a single line, Korean syllables are written in clusters or boxes. Each box can contain two, three, or sometimes four letters. The letters in these boxes are arranged from left to right and top to bottom. The syllables that form a word are placed right next to each other. Spaces separate words, as in English.

Take a look at the following box. to see how the letters in a syllable are read from left to right then top to bottom. Again, the word 김치 **kimchi** is displayed. This time, however, arrows show the order to follow in order when reading the letters. Read from left to right, maximum of two letters, then move to the lower line and again read from left to right. Then move to the next cluster and do the same. It's important to note that Koreans think of a word like 김치 **kimchi** as consisting of two syllables, not five letters.

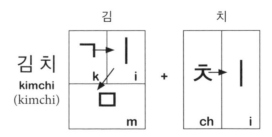

The next box displays a slightly more complicated Korean word 앉다 **anda**, which is the verb "to sit." Here, the first syllable has four letters which are read in the same pattern (left to right in the top row, then down and again from left to right in the bottom row and then move to the next syllable).

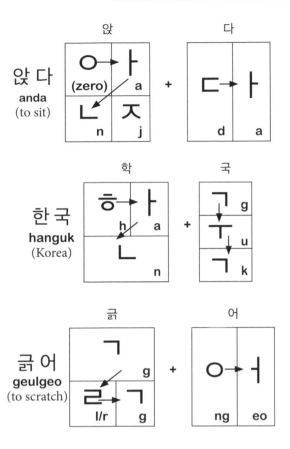

Every Korean syllable begins with a consonant. For example, the syllable 김 **kim** in 김치 **kimchi** starts with the letter ㄱ **g**, and the syllable 치 **chi** starts with the letter ㅊ **ch**. If a syllable begins with a vowel, the "zero consonant" ㅇ **ng** is used. The zero consonant means that this letter has no sound at the beginning of a word. For example, the letter ㅇ **ng** in 앉 **an** has no sound. The sound of the next letter ㅏ **a** is pronounced as the beginning sound of a syllable.

* **Note:** The vertical vowels such as ㅏ, ㅑ, ㅓ, ㅕ, ㅣ, are written to the right of the initial letter (e.g., 가, 펴, 니). However, the horizontal vowels, such as ㅗ, ㅛ, ㅜ, ㅠ, ㅡ, are written below the initial letter (e.g., 도, 슈, 츠).

🎧 Practice Activity 1: Writing Syllables in Hangeul

Look back at the consonant and vowel charts to review the letters and sounds, then try to sound out these syllables.

Practice writing the syllables as you read the letters out loud.

사 sa						
여 yeo						
류 ryu						
과 kwa						
워 wo						
돼 dwae						
핀 pin						
달 dal						
떡 ddeok						
흰 huin						
됐 dwaet						
웬 wen						

Practice Activity 2: Writing Hangeul Words

Practice reading and writing the following words that have syllables with vertical vowels, horizontal vowels and multiple consonants. Listen to the recordings and pronounce each word as you write it.

돼지 **dwaeji** (pig)								
쇠 **soe** (steel)								
흰색 **huinsaek** (white)								
왼쪽 **oenjjok** (left)								
물 **mul** (water)								
원하다 **wonhada** (to want)								
방 **bang** (room)								
이름 **ireum** (name)								
학생 **haksaeng** (student)								
뿔 **ppul** (horn)								

Sound Changes in Korean 🎧

Sound changes occur in every language where a sound in a word is influenced by other sounds in the word. For example, in English *Got you* is often pronounced as *Gotcha* and *let me* is pronounced as *lemme*; *kind of* as *kinda*. Although sound changes are not as common in Korean as in English, they are nevertheless an important aspect of Korean that you need to know in order to pronounce written Korean words correctly. This will be covered in detail in a later section. For now, simply note that a word's pronunciation in Korean usually, but not always, follows the spelling. But certain combinations of letters are not pronounced as they are written.

Here are some examples of sound changes in Korean:

English meanings	Changes in sounds
"thank you"	감사합니다 **gamsahapnida** is pronounced **gamsahamnida**
"to do"	합니다 **hapnida** is pronounced **hamnida**
"soup"	국물 **gukmul** is pronounced **gungmul**

1. If we pronounce this word exactly as it is spelled no one will understand us.
2. This is because there is a letter "ㅂ" **b** in this word that is not pronounced with its usual **b/p** sound.
3. Because of the influence of the following **n** sound, it is pronounced as an "ㅁ" **m**, causing 감사합니다 **gamsahapnida** to be pronounced "감사함니다 **gamsahamnida**." In the word **gamsahamnida** the "ㅂ" **b** sound is replaced by an "ㅁ" **m** sound.
4. Sound changes occur in many other words such as: "authority" 권력 **gwollyeok** (not **gwonryeok**), and "together" 같이 **gachi** (not **gati**).

As you learn new words, be sure to listen carefully to the readings of how they are pronounced and compare that to how they are spelled to help you recognize the sound changes.

Korean Word Order

You probably already know that the standard word order in English is **subject + verb + object** as in the sentence, "She ate breakfast." Korean word order is **subject + object + predicate (verb)** as in the sentence, "She breakfast ate." The subject or object must come first, and the predicate (verb) normally comes at the end of the sentence.

저	는	밥	을	먹	었	어	요
jeo	neun	bab	eul	meog	eoss	eo	yo
pronoun +	subject marker	noun +	object marker	verb stem +	past tense marker	+ word ending	
subject		object		predicate (verb)			
I		rice		ate			

Examples (subject: S, object: O, verb: V)

1. 마이크는(S) + 밥을(O) + 먹었어요(V). **Maikeuneun babeul meogeosseoyo.**
   Mike   + a meal + had ➠ *Mike had a meal.*

2. 우리는(S) + 한국에(O) + 가요(V). **Urineun hanguge gayo.**
   We   + to Korea + go ➠ *We go to Korea.*

3. 그는(S) + 영화를(O) + 좋아해요(V). **Geuneun yeonghwareul joahaeyo.**
   He   + movies   + like ➠ *He likes movies.*

4. 한국이(S) + 우승을(O)   + 했습니다(V). **Hangugi useungeul haetseumnida.**
   Korea   + the championship + won ➠ *Korea won the championship.*

Korean Particles

Particles, which are the equivalents in Korean to English prepositions (*in, on, over, under*, etc.), occur after their associated elements. For example, in English we would say, "to school." But in Korean we say, "school to."

However, Korean particles also mark the function of words in a sentence such as subjects, objects, possessives, and others.

1. Subject particles such as 이 **i** and 가 **ga** show that the preceding word is the subject of the sentence.

   민수가 학생입니다.   **Minsuga haksaengimnida.**   *Minsu is a student.*

   한국이 이겼습니다.   **Hangugi igyeotseumnida.**   *Korea won.*

2. Object particles such as 을 **eul** and 를 **reul** are used to show which word is the object of the sentence.

   민수가 나를 사랑합니다.   **Minsuga nareul saranghamnida.**   *Minsu loves me.*

   한국이 게임을 이겼습니다.   **Hangugi geimeul igyeotseumnida.**
   Korea won the game.

3. The possessive marker 의 **eui** generally expresses a possessive relationship between two words.

    정기<u>의</u> 차는 흰색입니다.   **Jeonggiui chaneun huinsaegimnida.**
    Jeongki's car is white.

    이것은 내 친구<u>의</u> 가방입니다.   **Igeoseun nae chinguui gabangimnida.**
    This is my friend's bag.

Modifiers

Korean is a **modifier + head** language which means that modifying elements or words come before the things modified, as in English.

For example in the phrase, 큰 가방 **keun kabang** (big bag), we can see that "big" comes before "bag" just as it does in English and many other languages. Another example is, 만난 친구 **mannan chingu** (the friend I met). This is slightly different from English and literally translates into "the met friend." In this case, the modifier "met" comes before the element it modifies which is "friend."

There are several ways to modify nouns:

1. **Using a modifier**
    A modifier's basic function is to modify nouns, as in: 새 구두 **sae gudu** (new shoes). 새 **Sae** is a modifier that describes the condition of 구두 **gudu**.

    Other examples:
    그 구두 **geu gudu** (those shoes)
    여러 집 **yeoreo jip** (many houses)
    대 사건 **dae sageon** (a big event)
    새 차 **sae cha** (a new car)

2. **Using a modifying marker "의" ui**
    The modifying marker 의 **ui** enables nouns and pronouns to modify other nouns, as in: 나의 차 **naui cha** (my car).
    By using 의 **ui**, the meaning of the word 나 **na** changes from "I" into "my."

    Other examples:
    나의 손 **naui son** (my hands)
    아빠의 차 **appaui cha** (father's car)
    나의 집 **naui jip** (my house)
    오늘의 요리 **oneurui yori** (today's menu)

3. **Using a noun + noun combination**
    Nouns can modify other nouns when they come in the modifier's position, as in: 회사 차 **hoesa cha** (company's car).

Other examples:
친구 구두 **chingu gudu** (a friend's shoes)
한국 차 **hanguk cha** (a Korean car)
고양이 손 **goyangi son** (cat hands)
사기 사건 **sagi sageon** (a fraud case)

4. **Using an inflector**
   Verbs and adjectives can be turned into a modifier by using inflectors. One of the inflectors frequently used is "-ㄴ" **n**, as in 고친 집 **gochin jip** (fixed house). 고치다 **Gochida** is originally a verb, but it can modify a noun by using the inflector "-ㄴ" **n**.

   Other examples:
   헌 집 **heon jip** (an old house)
   큰 구두 **keun gudu** (big shoes)
   깨끗한 손 **kkaekkeutan son** (clean hands)
   빠른 차 **ppareun cha** (a fast car)

Flexible Word Order in Korean

As we have seen, the subject in Korean appears at the beginning of a sentence, and the object follows it. Interestingly, though, as long as the predicate (verb) remains at the end of the sentence, the order of the other words can be scrambled for various purposes (to emphasize one thing over another).

For example, the meaning of a sentence "I love you" can be kept even though the subject and the object are scrambled.

1. 영수가   미나를   사랑해
   Yeongsuga   Minareul   saranghae.
   YeongSu   Mina   love
   YeongSu loves Mina.

2. 미나를   영수가   사랑해.
   Minareul   Yeongsuga   saranghae.
   Mina   YeongSu   love
   YeongSu loves Mina.

For example, you might say, "I to John the apple gave" or you could also say, "I the apple to John gave." Both are correct and it just depends on whether you want to place more emphasis on John (the recipient) or on the apple (what was given to him). Below are a couple of additional examples.

1. 영수가   미나에게   사과를   주었다.
   Yeongsuga   Minaege   sagwareul   jueotda.
   YeongSu   to-Mina   an apple   gave
   YeongSu gave an apple to Mina.

2. 영수가   사과를   미나에게   주었다
   Yeongsuga   sagwaeul   Minaege   jueotda.
   YeongSu   an apple   to-Mina   gave
   YeongSu gave an apple to Mina.

🎧 **Practice Activity 3:** Sentence Writing Practice

Practice reading and writing the following sentences. Pay attention to the word order, syllables, vertical and horizontal vowels and multiple consonants. Listen to the recordings and pronounce the sentences aloud several times as you write them.

1. **Hello. / Annyeonghaseyo.**

안	녕	하	세	요.
an	**nyeong**	**ha**	**se**	**yo**

2. **She is kind. / Geunyeoneun chakhamnida.**

그	녀	는	착	합	니	다.
geu	**nyeo**	**neun**	**chak**	**ham**	**ni**	**da**
she + subject marker			(is) kind + word ending.			

3. **I am American. / Jeoneun miguk saramimnida.**

저	는	미	국	사	람	입	니	다.
jeo	**neun**	**mi**	**guk**	**sa**	**ram**	**im**	**ni**	**da**
I + subj. marker		American (am) + word ending.						

4. He went to Korea. / Keuneun hanguge gasseoyo.

그	는	한	국	에	갔	어	요.
keu	neun	han	gug	e	gass	eo	yo
he + subj. marker		Korea (to) + obj. marker			went + word ending.		

5. I hit him. / Naneun geureul ttaeryeosseoyo.

나	는	그	를	때	렸	어	요.
na	neun	geu	reul	ttae	ryeoss	eo	yo
I + subj. marker		him + obj. marker		hit + word ending.			

Review Questions
1. Does the Korean language use ideographs or an alphabet?
2. How are Korean letters and words organized?
3. Do Korean letters always make the basic sound they are assigned?
4. Does Korean have particles equivalent to English prepositions?
5. What is the basic word order in Korean?

LESSON 1
Greetings and Essential Expressions

This chapter will be of immediate benefit to all learners and is geared especially to those who will visit Korea and need to know certain critical phrases. While most of the cities in Korea are teeming with English on signs, menus and advertisements, this vocabulary-rich introductory section will help you to communicate by providing basic expressions for getting around, interacting with Koreans, visiting popular destinations, buying electronics, and conducting simple transactions such as ordering food or paying for things at a cash register.

🎧 ESSENTIAL PHRASES 1　Hello and Goodbye

Hello!	안녕하세요! **Annyeonghaseyo!**
It's nice to meet you.	반갑습니다. **Bangapseumnida.**
I am [name].	저는 [__] 입니다. **Jeoneun [___] imnida.**
Hello? (On the phone)	여보세요? **Yeoboseyo?**
Take care! (Lit. "Go well")	잘 가요! **Jal gayo!**
Goodbye. (to someone leaving)	안녕히 가세요. **Annyeonghi gaseyo.**
Goodbye. (to someone staying when you leave)	안녕히 계세요. **Annyeonghi gyeseyo.**

🎧 New Vocabulary 1

yes	네, 예 **ne, ye**
no	아니요 **aniyo**
I	저, 나 **jeo, na**
you	당신, 너 **dangsin, neo**
he, she, they	그, 그녀, 그들 **geu, geunyeo, geudeul**
us	저희, 우리 **jeoheui, uri**
you all	여러분 **yeoreobun**
man	남자 **namja**
woman	여자 **yeoja**
who	누구 **nugu**
what	무엇 **mueot**
when	언제 **eonjae**
where	어디 **eodi**
why	왜 **wae**
how	어떻게 **eotteoke**
here	여기 **yeogi**

there	거기 **geogi**
over there	저기 **jeogi**
Mr./Mrs. ~	~씨 **~ssi**

Practice Activity 1: Writing Names in Hangeul

Use the spaces below to copy some of the Hangeul phrases above. Then using the information from the Introduction (pp. 7-8), try to spell out your name in romanized Korean and use it to introduce yourself. Here are some examples of western names that have been spelled with Korean letters.

Bailey	배일리	**Baeilli**
Carolyn	캐럴린	**Kaereollin**
Jessie	제시	**Jesi**
Natalie	나탈리	**Natalli**
Savannah	사바나	**Sabana**
Jason	제이슨	**Jeiseun**
Michael	마이클	**Maikeul**
Todd	토드	**Todeu**
Devon	데번	**Debeon**
Steve	스티브	**Seutibeu**

Korean Sentence Structure

In English, the typical sentence structure is **subject + verb + object**. "Jim read a book." In Korean, the sentence structure follows a **subject + object + verb** format as in, "Jim + a book + read."

While this will be addressed further in later chapters, here are some sample sentences to introduce you to Korean sentence structure followed by some common greetings and farewells.

대성이	은행에	갔다.
Daeseongi	**eunhaenge**	**gatda**
Daeseong	*the bank to*	*went.*
noun+subj. marker	object+particle	verb+ending

지나가	제 스마트폰을	봤나요?
Jinaga	**je seumateuponeul**	**bwannayo?**
Jina	*my smartphone*	*saw?*
noun+subj. marker	object+obj. marker	verb+ending

제가	버스를	오랫동안	기다렸습니다.
Jega	**beoseureul**	**oraetdongan**	**gidaryeotseumnida.**
I	*the bus*	*for a long time*	*waited.*
noun+subj. marker	object+ obj. marker	adverb+time word	verb+ending

CULTURAL NOTE ## Speech Levels and Addressing Others

In Korean, there are varying levels of speech, which will be covered in more detail in the next chapter. The three most commonly utilized levels are low form, middle form (sometimes referred to as polite form), and high form.

Most sentences in this book are written in middle form which is the polite everyday form most appropriate for all levels of societal communication.

It's nice to meet you.
Bangawoyo.

The higher the form, the more respectful you are being to the person you are speaking to. It's important to understand where you fit in the social hierarchy (to be discussed later in this book) in order to understand what forms to use when speaking to different people. To simplify:

• **Low form** is for very close friends or for those whose social status is lower than yours or who are younger than you.
• **Middle form** is most appropriate for polite everyday communication with people from all social levels. For example, you use it when speaking to work colleagues, the cashier at the grocery store, and acquaintances.

• **High form** is used mainly in formal contexts or to address those who are older or more senior to you (starting with age) such as the elderly, company heads, school teachers or principals, or someone who deserves a great amount of respect.

Common Forms of Address

Koreans rarely use the word "you" when addressing someone. In the New Vocabulary list above, the word 당신 **dangsin** is only used among spouses or very close friends and would seem too aggressive to use with a stranger.

When referring to people you are speaking to, it is more polite to refer to them by their first name or full name followed by 씨 **ssi**, such as, "Lisa **ssi**."

Some other forms of address are 아/ 야 (**a/ ya**) used after the first name. This is used the same way as 씨 (**ssi**), but it denotes someone who is close to you. 님 (**nim**) functions like **ssi** but is attached at the end of someone's title to show respect.

Examples

Namjeong	남정 씨	**Namjeong ssi**
Bak Namjeong	박남정 씨	**BakNamjeong ssi**
Taehyeong	태형아	**Taehyeonga**
Minsu	민수야	**Minsuya**
Manager	과장님	**gwajangnim**
Teacher	선생님	**seonsaengnim**

 ┊ESSENTIAL PHRASES 2┊   **"Thank You" and "Excuse Me"**

Thank you.	고맙습니다.	**Gomapseumnida.**
Thank you very much.	감사합니다.	**Gamsahamnida.**
I'm sorry.	미안합니다.	**Mianhamnida.**
I'm so sorry.	죄송합니다.	**Joesonghamnida.**
Perhaps.	혹시.	**Hoksi.**
Excuse me.	실례합니다.	**Sillyehamnida.**
Pardon me/just a moment.	잠시만요.	**Jamsimanyo.**
Do you speak English?	영어 하세요?	**Yeongeo haseyo?**
I don't understand.	이해 못해요.	**Ihae mothaeyo.**
I don't speak Korean well...	한국말을 잘 못합니다.	
	Hangungmareul jal mothamnida.	
Please speak slowly.	천천히 말해주세요.	
	Cheoncheonhi malhaejuseyo.	
Can you write that down?	그거 써 주세요.	**Geugeo sseo juseyo.**
Can you text it to me?	그거 문자로 저한테 보내주세요.	
	Geugeo munjaro jeohante bonaejuseyo.	

How do you say [English word] in Korean?	한국어로 _____ 어떻게 말해요? **Hangugeoro _____ eotteoke malhaeyo?**
What is this called in Korean?	이거 한국어로 뭐라고 해요? **Igeo hangugeoro mworago haeyo?**
Where is the bathroom?	화장실이 어디예요? **Hwajangsiri eodiyeyo?**

New Vocabulary 2

Thank you.	고맙습니다.	**Gomapseumnida.**
Thank you very much.	감사합니다.	**Gamsahamnida.**
I'm sorry.	미안합니다.	**Mianhamnida.**
I'm so sorry.	죄송합니다.	**Joesonghamnida.**
Perhaps.	혹시.	**Hoksi.**
Excuse me.	실례합니다.	**Sillyehamnida.**

CULTURAL NOTE   How to say "Excuse me!" in Korean

"**Hoksi**, do you speak English?" This helpful word **hoksi** (혹시) is a fantastic way of getting someone's attention in Korean. It is an icebreaker that takes the place of the phrase "Excuse me" in English when trying to start a conversation with someone.

Jamsimanyo (잠시만요) is another word used to express "Excuse me" but it differs from **hoksi** in its usage. While it might get someone's attention, it is more often used with a short chopping motion of the hand to indicate that you are trying to squeeze past someone. It literally means "just a moment" and informs those around you that the inconvenient jostling and pushing will be over momentarily.

실례합니다 **Sillyehamnida** can also be translated as "Excuse me!" but it is used in more formal situations. For example, asking people to take a survey, visiting new places, or entering a store to ask for a favor.

Excuse me!
Jamsimanyo!

These three expressions are somewhat interchangeable.

Examples
1. Asking something (*on a road to random people*)
   i) 실례합니다. 이것 좀 부탁드립니다.
   Sillyehamnida. Igeot jom butakdeurimnida. *Excuse me. Can you do this?*
   ii) 실례지만 설문 조사 좀 부탁드립니다.
   Sillyejiman seolmun josa jom butakdeurimnida.
   Excuse me. Can you take a survey?

2. Visiting new places
   i) 실례합니다. 여기 사진관 맞죠? **Sillyehamnida. Yeogi sajingwan matjyo?**
      Excuse me. Is this a photo studio?
   ii) 실례지만 컴퓨터를 사러 왔는데요.
      Sillyejiman keompyuteoreul sareo wanneundeyo.
      Excuse me. I'm here to buy a computer

3. Asking for a favor (*inside a store to a clerk*)
   i) 실례합니다. 명동에 어떻게 가야 돼요?
      Sillyehamnida. Myeongdonge eotteoke gaya dwaeyo?
      Excuse me. How can I get to Myeongdong?

   ii) 실례지만 충전 좀 할 수 있을까요?
      Sillyejiman chungjeon jom hal su isseulkkayo?
      Excuse me. Can I charge my phone here?

Practice Activity 2: "Thank you" and "Excuse Me" Exercise

Without looking back at your essential phrases can you write the following, conjugated words in English?

1. 죄송합니다 _____

2. 감사합니다 _____

3. 실례합니다 _____

4. 혹시 _____

🎧 ESSENTIAL PHRASES 3   Asking Questions

Please help!	도와주세요!	**Dowajuseyo!**
Can I use the phone?	전화 좀 쓸 수 있어요?	**Jeonhwa jom sseul su isseoyo?**
I have a question.	질문이 있어요.	**Jilmuni isseoyo.**
What time is it?	몇 시예요?	**Myeot siyeyo?**
Just a moment...	잠깐만요...	**Jamkkanmanyo...**
Really?	진짜요?	**Jinjjayo?**
I understand.	알겠습니다.	**Algetseumnida.**
I know.	알아요.	**Arayo.**
I don't know.	몰라요.	**Mollayo.**

GRAMMAR NOTE   "To Be" vs "To Exist" in Korean

Here are two words that you will use often: 이다 **ida** (to be), and 있다 **itda** (to exist) (이에요 **ieyo** or 있어요 **isseoyo** in polite form). Both of these words can be translated to mean "to be"; however, the latter, 있다 **itda**, more specifically means, "to exist." These words are not interchangeable.

"To be" 이다 ida
I am a student. 나는 학생이다. **Naneun haksaengida.**
She is a doctor.   그녀는 의사이다. **Geunyeoneun uisaida.**
He is a manager at the store.
그는 상점의 점장이다. **Geuneun sangjeomui jeomjangida.**

"To exist" 있다 itda
Seoul is in Korea. 서울은 한국에 있다. **Seoureun hanguge itda.**
I have a bicycle.   나는 자전거가 있다. **Naneun jajeongeoga itda.**
I am in a hospital now.
나는 지금 병원에 있다. **Naneun jigeum byeongwone itda.**

When a person introduces themselves, they use 이다 **ida**.

"저는 캐서린 이에요" **Jeoneun Catherine ieyo.** (I am Catherine).

When someone says, "that is a dog" they would also use 이다 **ida**,

"저것은 개예요" **Jeogeoseun gaeyeyo.**

because it describes something, perhaps a trait, a name, or a state of being concerning the subject. 이에요 **Ieyo** turns into its short form 예요 **yeyo** when a preceding syllable ends in a vowel as shown in "개예요" **gaeyeyo**.

How is 있다 **itda** different from 이다 **ida**?
When stating something exists, we tend to say "he/she/it is somewhere." **Geudeureun chae isseoyo.** 그들은 차에 있어요. (They exist in [the] car.) Additionally, 있다 **itda** can be used to say that something is in one's possession. "I have a key." **Jeoege yeolsoega isseoyo** (저에게 열쇠가 있어요), and "Do you have a tissue?" **Hyujiga isseoyo?** (휴지가 있어요?) are both examples of how to appropriately use 있다 **itda**.

Common Locations

bank	은행 **eunhaeng**	
bus stop/bus station	버스 정류장 **beoseu jeongnyujang**	
church	교회 **gyohoe**	
embassy	대사관 **daesagwan**	
grocery store/mart	식료품 점/마트 **singnyopum jeom/mateu**	
hospital	병원 **byeongwon**	
hotel	호텔 **hotel**	

house/home	집 **jip**
apartment building	아파트 **apateu**
coffee shop	커피 숍 **keopi syop**
metro/subway station	지하철 역 **jihacheol yeok**
post office	우체국 **ucheguk**
police station	경찰서 **gyeongchalseo**
school	학교 **hakgyo**
restaurant	식당 **sikdang**

Places in South Korea

Seoul Station (a train station) 서울 역 **Seoul yeok**
Hongdae (an art and entertainment district of Seoul) 홍대 **Hongdae**
Myeongdong (a shopping area) 명동 **Myeongdong**
Gyeongbokgung Palace 경복궁 **Gyeongbokgung**
Gangnam (Seoul's upscale neighborhood) 강남 **Gangnam**
Jeju Island (a tourist destination with beaches and resorts) 제주도 **Jejudo**
Busan City (South Korea's second largest city) 부산 시 **Busan si**
Insadong (shops, teahouses and eateries) 인사동 **Insa Dong**
Dongdaemun Market 동대문 시장 **Dongdaemun sijang**
Namdaemun Market 남대문 시장 **Namdaemun sijang**
Seodaemun Market 서대문 시장 **Seodaemun sijang**
N Seoul Tower 서울타워 N **Seoul Tawo N**
Itaewon 이태원 **Itaewon**
Cheonggyecheon 청계천 **Cheonggyecheon**
Bukchon Hanok Village 북촌 한옥 마을 **Bukchon hanok maeul**
The DMZ 비무장 지대 **Bimujang jidae**

Practice Activity 3: Asking Directions in Korean

Think of a place and practice asking directions to that place.

_____ **eun/neun eodie isseoyo?**
(insert location)

"_____" 은/는 어디에 있어요?

Practice writing sentences in Hangeul using 있다 **itda** (to exist). Be sure to utilize the vocabulary and phrases learned previously in this section.

Where is So Yuna?

SoYunaneun eodie isseoyo?

소유나는 어디에 있어요?

Use this sentence structure:		
Subject +	Place +	**isseoyo**
eun/neun +	**e** +	**isseoyo**
은/는 +	에 +	있어요?
So Yuna +	post office at +	is
SoYunaneun +	**ucheguge** +	**isseoyo**
소유나는 +	우체국에 +	있어요.

Where is Ryan?

Raieoneun eodie isseoyo?

라이언은 어디에 있어요?

Where is Gilly?

Gillineun eodie isseoyo?

길리는 어디에 있어요?

Where is Eric?

Erigeun eodie isseoyo?

에릭은 어디에 있어요?

Where is Miyanko?

Miyankoneun eodie isseoyo?

미얀코는 어디에 있어요?

LESSON 2
Shopping in Korea

🎧 **ESSENTIAL PHRASES 1** **Eating Out in Korea**

Do you take credit/debit cards?	카드 돼요? **Kadeu dwaeyo?**
Please give me a *Gimbap*.	김밥 주세요. **Gimbap juseyo.**
Please give me a burger.	버거 주세요. **Beogeo juseyo.**
Please give me water.	물 주세요. **Mul juseyo.**
Do you have a table?	자리 있어요? **Jari isseoyo?**
I would like _____.	____ 주세요. _____ **juseyo.**
Please give me one like that.	저거랑 같은 거 주세요. **Jeogeorang gateun geo juseyo.**
One more please.	하나 더 주세요. **Hana deo juseyo.**
Over here!	여기요. **Yeogiyo!**
I have an allergy.	알러지가 있어요. **Alleojiga isseoyo.**
Please don't make it spicy.	안 맵게 해주세요. **An maepge haejuseyo.**
I will eat well!	잘먹겠습니다! **Jalmeokgaetseumnida!**
I ate well!	잘먹었습니다! **Jalmeogeotseumnida!**
This is delicious!	맛있어요! **Masisseoyo!**
This doesn't taste good.	맛이 없어요. **Masi eopseoyo.**

🎧 **New Vocabulary 1**

credit card	카드 **kadeu**
card payment only	카드전용 **kadejeonyong**
restaurant	음식점 **eumsikjeom**
coffeehouse	커피숍 **keopisyob**
cafe	카페 **kkape**
eatery	식당 **sigdang**
coke/soda	콜라/ 탄산음료 **kolla/tansaneumnyo**
coffee	커피 **keopi**
tea	차 **cha**
water	물 **mul**
ice cream	아이스크림 **aiseukeurim**
pizza	피자 **pija**
cake/pastry	케잌/제과 **keik/jegwa**
gimbap	김밥 **gimbap**
kimchi	김치 **gimchi**
bibimbap	비빔밥 **bibimbap**

hungry	배가 고파요	**baega gopayo**
thirsty	목이 말라요	**mogi mallayo**
how big a portion?	양이 얼마나 돼요?	**yangi eolmana dwaeyo?**
how much is it?	얼마예요	**eolmayeyo?**
delicious	맛있어요	**masisseoyo**
not delicious	맛이 없어요	**masi eopseoyo**
spicy	매워요	**maewoyo**
hot	뜨거워요	**tteugeowoyo**
cold	차가워요	**chagawoyo**

Practice Activity 1

Use the vocabulary in the box below in phrases to order food or to ask for an item.

Camera	카메라	**kamera**
Pizza	피자	**pija**
Ring	반지	**banji**
Tteokbokki	떡볶이	**tteokbokki**
Album	앨범	**aelbeom**
Banana Milk	바나나 우유	**banana uyu**
Ticket	표	**pyo**
Cola	콜라	**kolla**
Chocolate	초콜릿	**chokollit**
Hair Brush	헤어 브러시	**heeo beureosi**

Examples:
1. 짜장면 주세요. **Jjajangmyeon juseyo.** (Please give me *jjajangmyeon.*)

2. 머리끈 있어요? **Meorikkeun isseoyo?** (Do you have hair ties?)

_____

_____

_____

🎧 ⌈ESSENTIAL PHRASES 2⌉ Shopping in Korea

Do you have..?	_____ 있어요? _____ isseoyo?
How much is this?	이거 얼마예요? Igeo eolmayeyo?
Is there a bigger size?	더 큰 사이즈 있어요 Deo keun saijeu isseoyo?
Please give me this.	이거 주세요 Igeo juseyo.

New Vocabulary 2

shopping center	쇼핑 센터	syoping senteo
market	시장	sijang
pharmacy	약국	yakguk
bookstore	서점	seojeom
bakery	빵집	bbangjib
open	영업중	yeongeopjung
closed	영업종료	yeongeopjongnyo
open hours	영업시간	yeongeopsigan
red	빨강	ppalgang
yellow	노랑	norang
orange	주황	juhwang
blue	파랑	parang
green	연두	yeondu
white	하양	hayang
black	검정	geomjeong
pink	분홍	bunhong
big	큰	keun
small	작은	jageun
medium	중간	junggan
cheap	싼	ssan
expensive	비싼	bissan
discount	할인	harin
sales	세일	seil
clothing	의류	euiryu
menswear	남성의류	namseong euiryu
ladies' wear	숙녀의류	sungnyeo euiryu
shoes wear	구두/신발	gudu / sinbal
bags	가방	gabang
accessories	악세사리	aksesari
cashier counter	계산대	gyesandae
cashless payment	카드 결제	kadeu gyeolje
cash payment	현금 결제	hyeongeum gyeolje
QR scan	QR 스캔	kyual seukaen

Practice Activity 2

Use the vocabulary in the box below to ask where each place is. For example,

Where is the pharmacy? 약국이 어디 있어요? (**Yakgugi eodi isseoyo?**)

_____ 어디 있어요?

(_____ **eodi isseoyo?**)

쇼핑	시장	서점
센터	약국	빵집

Let's go to the market

Complete the crossword puzzle below by writing the Korean terms for the market in English.

Across
1. 카드
4. 비싸다
6. 신발
7. 택시
8. 싸다
9. 사다

Down
1. 옷
2. 돈
3. 식당
5. 약국

New Vocabulary 3

This section provides examples of vocabulary related to things we use daily such as cell phones, hygiene products, and internet. We have also included general vocabulary terms essential for travel; you may like to know words for technology and toiletries as they will prove useful.

Mobile Technology Terms

laptop 노트북 **noteubuk**
phone 전화 **jeonhwa**
cellular phone 휴대 전화 **hyudae jeonhwa**
charger 충전기 **chungjeongi**
charging cable 충전 케이블 **chungjeon keibeul**
data cable 데이터 케이블 **deiteo keibeul**
battery 건전지 **geonjeonji**
wireless charger 무선 충전기 **museon chungjeongi**
power outlet 전원 콘센트 **jeonwon konsenteu**
converter/adapter 컨버터/어댑터 **keonbeoteo/eodaepteo**
password 비밀 번호 **bimil beonho**

fingerprint scanner 지문 스캐너 **jimun seukaeneo**
facial recognition 안면 인식 **anmyeon insik**
iris scanner 홍채 스캐너 **hongchae seukaeneo**

on/off 켜기/끄기 **kyeogi/kkeugi**
locked/unlocked 잠금/잠금 해제 **jamgeum/jamgeum haejae**
open/close (an app) 열기/닫기 **yeolgi/datgi**
wireless 무선 **museon**
text message 문자 **munja**
picture 사진 **sajin**
Can you take a picture? 사진 찍어주세요. **Sajin jjigeojuseyo.**
selfie 셀카 **selka**
cartoon 만화 **manhwa**
emoji 이모티콘 **imotikon**
search 검색 **geomsaek**
flashlight 후레쉬 **hureswi**
night mode 야간 모드 **yagan modeu**
rotation 회전 **hoejeon**
portrait mode 세로 모드 **sero modeu**
landscape mode 가로 모드 **garo modeu**
settings 설정 **seoljeong**
Do Not Disturb mode 방해금지 모드 **banghaegeumji modeu**
location 위치 **wichi**

flash drive USB 메모리 **USB memori**
Call app 전화 앱 **jeonhwa aep**
contacts 연락처 **yeollakcheo**
reminders 알림 **allim**
calendar 달력 **dallyeok**
To Do List 작업관리 목록 **jageopgwalli mongnok**
clock 시계 **sigye**

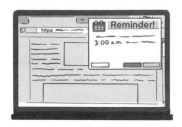

CULTURAL NOTE Selfie or Selka?

In Korea, the popularity of taking a selfie flourished even before the term "selfie" really took off in the West. Until having a quality camera built into your phone became the norm, Koreans used the term **selka** (a term derived from Self-Camera) which incorporated the term **dika** (a term derived from digital camera). This bit of digital slang is still in use today.

Basic Computer/Internet terms

operating system (OS) 오에스 **oeseu**
spreadsheet 스프레드쉬트 **seupeuredeuswiteu**
presentation 프레젠테이션 **peurejenteisyeon**
document 문서 **munseo**
confirm 승인 **seungin**
cancel 취소 **chwiso**
accept 수락 **surak**
reject 거부 **geobu**
okay 진행/확인 **jinhaeng/hwagin**
decline 거절 **geojeol**
add to cart 카트에 넣기 **kateue neoki**
checkout 계산 **gyesan**
payment method 결제 방법 **gyeolje bangbeop**
share 공유 **gongyu**
social media 소셜 미디어/SNS **sosyeol midieo/sns**
subscribe 구독 **gudok**
stream 스트림 **seuteurim**
bookmark 북마크 **bukmakeu**
back 뒤로 가기 **dwiro gagi**
forward 앞으로 가기 **apeuro gagi**
refresh 리프레쉬 **repeureswi**
open/close (a window) 열기/닫기 **yeolgi/datgi**

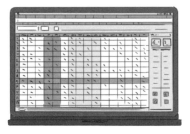

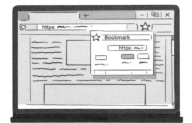

Toiletries and Other Travel Essentials

shampoo 샴푸 **shyampu**
conditioner 린스 **rinseu**
soap 비누 **binu**
body wash 바디워시 **badiwosi**
deodorant 데오도란트/탈취제 **deodoranteu/talchwijae**
lotion 로션 **rosyeon**
lip balm 립밤 **ripbam**
sunscreen 선크림 **seonkeurim**
moisturizer 보습제 **boseupje**
hand sanitizer 손 소독제 **son sodokje**
hair gel 젤/헤어젤 **jel/heeojel**
cologne/perfume 향수 **hyangsu**
toothbrush 칫솔 **chissol**
toothpaste 치약 **chiyak**
floss 치실 **chisil**
makeup 화장품 **hwajangpum**
makeup remover 메이크업 리무버/클렌징 **maeikeueob rimubeo/keullenjing**
foundation 파운데이션 **paundeisyeon**
lipstick 립스틱 **ripseutik**
eyeshadow 아이섀도 **aisyaedo**
mascara 마스카라 **maseukara**
blush 블러셔 **beuleosyeo**
eyeliner 아이라이너 **airaineo**
razor 면도기 **myeondogi**
shaving cream 쉐이빙 폼 **sweibing pom**
electric razor 전기 면도기 **jeongi myeondogi**
razor heads 면도날 **myeondonal**
aftershave 면도 크림/애프터 쉐이브 **myeondo keurim/aepeuteo sweibeu**
brush (롤) 빗 **(rol) bit**
comb 빗 **bit**
hair straightener 고데기/판 고데기 **godegi/pan godegi**
curling iron 고데기/컬링 아이언 **godegi/keolling aieon**
hair dryer 헤어 드라이어 **heeo deuraieo**
hair elastic 머리끈 **meorikkeun**
feminine hygiene 여성 용품 **yeoseong yongpum**
tampons 탐폰 **tampon**
pads 생리대 **saengnidae**
birth control 피임 **piim**
bandages 붕대/반창고 **bungdae/banchanggo**
Neosporin 연고 **yeongo**
alcohol wipe 알콜 솜 **alkol som**
pain relievers 진통제 **jintongje**

antacid 위장약/제산제 **wijangyak/jesanje**
prescription medication 처방약 **cheobangyak**
glasses 안경 **angyeong**
reading glasses 돋보기 **dotbogi**
contact lens 콘택트렌즈 **kontaekteu renjeu**
contact solution 콘택트렌즈 용액 **kontaekteu renjeu yongaek**
toilet paper 휴지 **hyuji**
wet tissue 물티슈 **multisyu**
tissue 티슈 **tisyu**
paper towel 키친 타월 **kichin tawol**
towel 수건/목욕 타월 **sugeon/mogyok tawol**
hand towel 수건 **sugeon**
wallet 지갑 **jigap**
purse 지갑 **jigap**
bag 가방 **gabang**
backpack 백팩 **baekpaek**
bank card 카드 **kadeu**
keys 열쇠 **yeolsoe**
ID 신분증 **sinbunjeung**
money 돈 **don**
passport 여권 **yeogwon**
clothes 옷 **ot**
shirt 셔츠 **sheocheu**
pants 바지 **baji**
skirt 치마 **chima**
dress 드레스/원피스 **deureseu/wonpiseu**
socks 양말 **yangmal**
coat 코트 **koteu**
shoes 신발 **sinbal**
underwear 속옷 **sogot**
hat 모자 **moja**
jewelry 악세사리/보석 **aksesari/boseok**

Practice Activity 3

Fill in the blanks with appropriate answers.

1. I want to buy _____ .

    _____ 사고 싶어요.

    _____ sago sipeoyo.

2. Do you have _____?

    _____ 있어요?

    _____ **isseoyo?**

3. Please give me _____ .

    _____ 주세요.

    _____ **juseyo.**

Hello! I'm Lauren. What is your name?

Annyeonghaseyo! Jeoneun Lorenieyo. Ireumi eotteoke doeseyo?

My name is Jisu. Nice to meet you. Do you take this class?

Je ireumeun Jisuyeyo. Bangapseumnida. I sueop deureuseyo?

Ah yes. I think this class will be fun! What is your major?

Ne. I sueobeun jaemiisseul geot gatayo! Jeongongi mwoyeyo?

Me too! Let's be friends.

Jeodoyo! Uri chinguhaeyo.

Biology. What about you?

Saengmulhagieyo. Loren ssineunyo?

LESSON 3
Introducing Yourself and Meeting Others

 DIALOGUE 1 **Making Friends**

College students, Lauren and Jisu, meet and decide to become friends.

Lauren: Hello! I'm Lauren. What is your name?
Annyeonghaseyo! Jeoneun Lorenieyo. Ireumi eotteoke doeseyo?
안녕하세요! 저는 로렌이에요. 이름이 어떻게 되세요?

Jisu: My name is Jisu. Nice to meet you. Do you take this class?
Je ireumeun Jisuyeyo. Bangapseumnida. I sueop deureuseyo?
제 이름은 지수예요. 반갑습니다. 이 수업 들으세요?

Lauren: Ah yes. I think this class will be fun! What is your major?
Ne. I sueobeun jaemiisseul geot gatayo! Jeongongi mwoyeyo?
네. 이 수업은 재미있을 것 같아요! 전공이 뭐예요?

Jisu: Biology. What about you?
Saengmulhagieyo. Loren ssineunyo?
생물학이에요. 로렌 씨는요?

Lauren: Me too! Let's be friends.
Jeodoyo! Uri chinguhaeyo.
저도요! 우리 친구해요.

New Vocabulary 1

name	이름 **ireum**
friend	친구 **chingu**
(to be) nice to meet	반갑다 **bangapda**
to hear, to take a class	듣다 **deutda**
to be	-이다 **ida**
class	수업 **sueop**
major	전공 **jeongong**
biology	생물학 **saengmulhak**
to be fun/interesting	재미있다 **jaemiitda**
to do	하다 **hada**

GRAMMAR NOTE   Topic Markers

The particles 은 **eun** and 는 **neun** are called topic markers because they are used to mark the topic of a sentence. These specific markers can be used to state general facts, show contrast, and introduce yourself. It is easy to think of these markers as a way to say "as for..." or "when it comes to... ."

For example, the sentence 저는 스시를 좋아해요 **jeoneun seusireul joahaeyo** can be translated as "As for me, I like sushi." Topic makers tell your audience what the topic of the sentence is. 은 **Eun** attaches to words ending in a consonant, as in 음식은 **eumsigeun**, and 는 **neun** comes after words ending with a vowel, as in 학교는 **hakgyoneun**.

1. **Stating general facts**
   학교는 공부를 하는 곳입니다.
   Hakgyoneun gongbureul haneun gosimnida.
   A school is a place for studying.

   음식은 사람을 행복하게 합니다.
   Eumsigeun sarameul haengbokage hamnida.
   Food makes people happy.

   그 사람은 똑똑합니다.
   Geu sarameun ttokttokamnida.
   He is smart.

2. **Showing contrast**
   이 차는 흰 색이지만 저 차는 검은색입니다.
   I chaneun huin saegijiman jeo chaneun geomeunsaegimnida.
   This car is white, but that car is black.

   오늘은 비가 오지만 내일은 맑을 겁니다.
   Oneureun biga ojiman naeireun malgeul geomnida.
   Today it is raining, but it'll be sunny tomorrow.

   저는 고기를 좋아하지만 제 아내는 야채를 좋아합니다.
   Jeoneun gogireul joahajiman je anaeneun yachaereul joahamnida.
   I like meat, but my wife likes vegetables.

3. **Introducing oneself**
   저는 가수입니다.
   Jeoneun gasuimnida.
   I'm a singer.

저<u>는</u> 한국 사람입니다.
Jeo<u>neun</u> hanguk saramimnida.
I'm Korean.

저<u>는</u> 한국 가수입니다.
Jeo<u>neun</u> hanguk gasuimnida.
I'm a Korean singer.

Lastly, consider the topic marker's role of showing contrast. To illustrate, examine the following example:

고기 먹어요?   **Gogi meogeoyo?**
Can you eat meat?

해물은 먹어요.   **Haemureun meogeoyo.**
(I can't eat meat, but) I eat seafood.

In this example, the phrase "I can't eat meat" is implied because of the speaker's use of 는 **neun**, the topic marker.

CULTURAL NOTE   How to Make Appropriate Introductions

Korean culture can seem to be very different from American culture. As such, it is important to know how to appropriately introduce yourself. Appropriate introductions all begin with a bow. The respect you are showing determines how deeply you bend down. In most cases, a slight tilt at the waist is sufficient. Next, depending on the formality of the introduction, it is appropriate to state your name and something like, "it is nice to meet you," or, in Korean: 반가워요 **bangawoyo**.

Practice Activity 1

Fill in the following blank spaces with appropriate markers, or words.

1. 안녕하세요. 저 _____ 영미예요. 반갑습니다.

   Annyeonghaseyo. Jeo _____ yeongmiyeyo. Bangapseumnida.

2. 안녕하세요. 제 이름 _____ 영미예요.

   Annyeonghaseyo. Je ireum _____ yeongmiyeyo.

3. 지수 씨 _____ 버거를 좋아해요.

   Jisu ssi _____ beogeoreul joahaeyo.

4. 대화 **daehwa** (conversation)

   a. 해물을 먹어요? **Haemureul meogeoyo?**

   b. 스시 _____ 먹어요. **Seusi _____ meogeoyo.**

5. 그 고양이_____ 부드러워요.

   Geu goyangi _____ budeureowoyo.

🎧 ┊DIALOGUE 2┊ **Where Are You From?**

Jisu and Lauren discuss where they are from.

Jisu: Which country are you from? Are you from America?
Eoneu naraeseo osyeosseoyo? Migugeseo wasseoyo?
어느 나라에서 오셨어요? 미국에서 왔어요?

Lauren: Yes, I'm from America and I am an international student at this school. Where are you from?
Ne, jeoneun migugeseo wasseoyo. I hakgyo yuhaksaengieyo. Eodieseo osyeosseoyo?
네, 저는 미국에서 왔어요. 이 학교 유학생이에요. 어디에서 오셨어요?

Jisu: Seoul is my hometown. I am also attending this school.
Jeoneun gohyangi Seoul-ieyo. Jeodo i hakgyoe danigo isseoyo.
저는 고향이 서울이에요. 저도 이 학교에 다니고 있어요.

🎧 **New Vocabulary 2**

which	어느	**eoneu**
country	나라	**nara**
to come	오다	**oda**
hometown	고향	**gohyang**
America	미국	**miguk**

international student	유학생 **yuhaksaeng**
where	어디 **eodi**
South Korea	한국 **hanguk**
school	학교 **hakgyo**
to attend	다니다 **danida**

GRAMMAR NOTE Answering "Yes" and "No"

The Korean words for "yes" and "no" have different meanings than in English depending on the context.

1. Statements of Agreement

When asked a yes or no question, the appropriate response is either 네 **ne** (yes), or 아니요 **aniyo** (no), depending upon whether or not you agree with the question. Examine the following example:

스시 안 좋아해요?   **Seusi an joahaeyo?**
−*You don't like sushi?*

네, 안 좋아해요.   **Ne, an joahaeyo.**
−*Yes, I don't like it.*

Here, 네 **ne** means "that's correct" or "I agree with that assessment." The same can be said of 아니요 **aniyo**. If you do like sushi, your response to the previous question would be 아니요, 좋아해요 **Aniyo, joahaeyo** "No, I do like sushi."

김치 안 먹어요? / 네.
Gimchi an meogeoyo? / Ne.
Do you not eat kimchi? / Yes. (I don't eat kimchi.)

김치 안 먹어요? / 아니요.
Gimchi an meogeoyo? / Aniyo.
Do you not eat kimchi? / No. (I eat kimchi.)

영화 좋아해요? / 네.
Yeonghwa joahaeyo? / Ne.
Do you like movies? / Yes. (I like movies.)

영화 좋아해요? / 아니요.
Yeonghwa joahaeyo? / Aniyo.
Do you like movies? / No. (I don't like movies.)

To enhance clarity, it is good practice to continue the sentence after stating your agreement or disagreement with the question.

2. As a Filler/Prompt in Conversations

In Korean, like in English, "yes" can be used as a prompt for the speaker to continue their thoughts. While having a conversation, it is common for English speakers to say things like "mm-hmm" or "right" in order to continue the conversation. In Korean it is the same. 네 **Ne** is used in such cases.

제가 어제 버스를 탔어요. / 네.
Jega eoje beoseureul tasseoyo. / Ne.
I took a bus yesterday. / Yes. (I'm listening. Go on.)

그런데 사고가 났어요. / 네.
Geureonde sagoga nasseoyo. / Ne.
But an accident occurred. / Yes. (I'm listening. Go on.)

그래서 경찰이 왔어요. / 네.
Geuraeseo gyeongchari wasseoyo. / Ne.
So the police came. / Yes. (I'm listening. Go on.)

3. As a Question Prompt

네 **Ne** can also stand alone, as a question, with rising intonation. In such a case, it means "what?" or "excuse me?"

큰 사고가 났어요. / 네?
Keun sagoga nasseoyo. / Ne?
A big accident occurred. / What? (Can you explain more?)

비행기가 안 온대요. / 네?
Bihaenggiga an ondaeyo. / Ne?
The plane is not coming. / What? (Can you tell me more?)

열쇠를 잃어버렸어요. / 네?
Yeolsoereul ireobeoryeosseoyo. / Ne?
I lost my key. / What? (So, what's the plan?)

CULTURAL NOTE Bowing and Shaking Hands

As discussed in the previous cultural notes, bowing is a polite gesture when making introductions. Shaking hands is also a common gesture but is often used between men to show respect. In Western cultures a handshake is done with one arm outstretched. In Korea, however, it is done with your left hand supporting your right forearm in order to show respect. Using two hands to shake the other person's hand is also acceptable.

Practice Activity 2

Fill in the following blanks with appropriate words and responses.

1. 어디에서 _____?

   Eodieseo _____?

2. 저는 _____ 에서 왔어요.

   Jeoneun _____ eseo wasseoyo.

3. 대화 **daehwa** (conversation)

   a. 오늘 고향에 안 가요?   **Oneul gohyange an gayo?**

   b. 네. _____.   **Ne. _____.**

4. 대화 **daehwa** (conversation)

   a. 학교 다니고 있어요?   **Hakgyo danigo isseoyo?**

   b. 아니요. _____.   **Aniyo. _____.**

5. _____ 나라에서 오셨어요?

   _____ **naraeseo osyeosseoyo?**

🎧 :DIALOGUE 3: **Meeting Someone Older**

Jihyun runs into an older man whom she already knows and he asks her if she is exercising.

Jihyeon: Hello, sir.
           Seonsaengnim, annyeonghasimnikka?
           선생님, 안녕하십니까?

Seoghun: Yes, nice seeing you here. How are you doing?
           Ne. Bangawoyo. Jal jinaejyo?
           네. 반가워요. 잘 지내죠?

Jihyeon: I'm doing good. I haven't seen you in such a long time. Nice to
           see you.
           Ne. Oraenmane boeni jeongmal bangapseumnida.
           네. 오랜만에 뵈니 정말 반갑습니다.

Seoghun: Yes. Are you still exercising these days?
           Geuraeyo. Yojeumdo undong haeyo?
           그래요. 요즘도 운동 해요?

Jihyeon: Yes. I want to do it every day, but it's not easy.
           Ne. Maeil hago sipeunde swipji anayo.
           네. 매일 하고 싶은데 쉽지 않아요.

Seoghun: Oh, I see. Being healthy is one of the most important things. You
           should try to exercise every day.
           **A, geuraeyo. Geongangi jeil jungyohaeyo. Kkok maeil undongeul
           haseyo.**
           아, 그래요. 건강이 제일 중요해요. 꼭 매일 운동을 하세요.

Jihyeon: Okay. I got it. Thank you.
           Ne. Algetseumnida. Gamsahamnida.
           네. 알겠습니다. 감사합니다.

🎧 New Vocabulary 3

to spend, to live	지내다 **jinaeda**
long time (long time no see)	오랜만이다 **oraenmanida**
high form for the word "to meet"	뵈다 **boeda**
exercise	운동 **undong**
every day	매일 **maeil**
easy	쉽다 **swipda**
health	건강 **geongang**
important	중요하다 **jungyohada**
to know	알다 **alda**

to not be (preceded by a verb)	-지 않다 **ji anta**
high form verb ending	-습니다 **sumnida**

GRAMMAR NOTE   **Negative Expressions**

The most common negative expressions used in Korean are:

-지 못하다   **ji motada**   *can't do*
-지 않다   **ji anta**   *won't do*

Both are used under different circumstances to express negatives in speech. They can also be shortened and used in front of verbs in this way:

제가 너무 바빠서 못 했어요.
Jega neomu bappaseo <u>mot</u> haesseoyo.
I was so busy I couldn't do it.

제가 공부를 안 했어요.
Jega gongbureul <u>an</u> haesseoyo.
I didn't study. (Because I didn't want to.)

When -지 않다 **ji anta** is used after verbs it means "do not."

For example:

농구를 좋아하는데 자주 하지 않아요.
Nonggureul joahaneunde jaju haji anayo.
I like basketball but I don't do it often.

In this example, and whenever 안 **an** is used, the negative expression indicates the subject's *choice* to play basketball infrequently, whereas -지 못하다 **ji motada** expresses the subject's *inability* to play basketball.

More examples of "-ji anta" sentences:

나는 농구를 하지 않는다.
Naneun nonggureul haji anneunda.
I don't play basketball. (Because I don't want to.)

사라는 공부를 하지 않는다.
Saraneun gongbureul haji anneunda.
Sarah doesn't study. (Because she is lazy, or enjoys playing rather than studying.)

If you use 안하다 **anhada** (you *choose* not to do something) in a situation where 못하다 **motada** (you *can't* do something) should be used, the audience may be offended by your choice to not do something.

More examples of "**-ji motada**" sentences:

나는 농구를 하지 못한다.
Naneun nonggureul haji motanda.
I can't play basketball. (Because I'm injured, or someone told me not to play basketball.)

사라는 공부를 하지 못한다.
Saraneun gongbureul haji motanda.
Sarah can't study. (Because she doesn't have a study room, or someone told her not to study.)

It is important to know the distinction between these two negative expressions. Since negatives can be a bit complicated in Korean, we will discuss them in more detail in Lesson 8.

CULTURAL NOTE   **Using Different Forms of Speech**

As we discussed in Lesson 1, in Korean, language is used to indicate levels of respect towards the audience. In the dialogue above, the 선생님 **seonsaengnim** (석훈 **seokoon**), or middle-aged man, is given more respect by the younger speaker because he is older. The younger speaker used more formal verb endings as well as 시 **si** and other softeners which indicate respect. In turn, the 선생님 **seonsaengnim** spoke middle level to the younger woman. However, the 선생님 **seonsaengnim** could have chosen to speak 반말 **banmal** or low form to the woman. As a rule, always speak higher forms of Korean to those older or of higher ranking than you.

Practice Activity 3

Fill in the following blanks with an appropriate negative expression.

1. 어제 잠을 많이 자서 오늘 피곤하지 _____ .

   Eoje jameul mani jaseo oneul pigonhaji _____ .

2. 선생님이 기분이 좋지 _____ .

   Seonsaengnimi gibuni jochi _____ .

3. 어제 피곤해서 운동을 _____ 했어요.

   Eoje pigonhaeseo undongeul _____ haesseoyo.

4. 요즘 바빠서 친구를 만나지 _____ 했어요.

   Yojeum bappaseo chingureul mannaji _____ haesseoyo.

5. 저는 농구를 _____ 해요.

   Jeoneun nonggureul _____ haeyo.

Should we eat lunch at 12?

Yeoldusie jeomsimeul meogeulkkayo?

Sounds good! But what time do we have to be at Hongdae? Today is WonJin's birthday party.

Joayo! Geureonde uriga myeotsikkaji hongdaee gaya dwaeyo? Oneul wonjini saengilpatiga itjanayo.

Ah that's right, WonJin said to be there by 3!

A, majayo, wonjiniga sesikkaji orago haesseoyo!

Sounds good. By the way, I also have an appointment at 7.

Joayo. Geureonde jega ilgopsiedo yaksogi isseoyo.

Okay! Then let's eat lunch and head straight to Hongdae!

Geuraeyo! Geureom jeomsim meokgo baro hongdaero gapsida!

Good plan!

Joayo!

Then, once the party ends, we can ride the subway over.

Geureom patiga kkeunnago jihacheoreul tago gamyeon dwaeyo.

LESSON 4
A Day In Seoul, My Schedule

🎧 ┊ DIALOGUE 1 ┊ **Planning My Day**

JiYoon and MinJun plan their day.

MinJun:	Should we eat lunch at 12?
	Yeoldusie jeomsimeul meogeulkkayo?
	12시에 점심을 먹을까요?
JiYoon:	Sounds good! But what time do we have to be at Hongdae? Today is WonJin's birthday party.
	Joayo! Geureonde uriga myeotsikkaji hongdaee gaya dwaeyo? Oneul wonjini saengilpatiga itjanayo.
	좋아요! 그런데 우리가 몇시까지 홍대에 가야 돼요? 오늘 원진이 생일파티가 있잖아요.
MinJun:	Ah that's right, WonJin said to be there by 3!
	A, majayo, wonjiniga sesikkaji orago haesseoyo!
	아, 맞아요, 원진이가 3시까지 오라고 했어요!
JiYoon:	Okay! Then let's eat lunch and head straight to Hongdae!
	Geuraeyo! Geureom jeomsim meokgo baro hongdaero gapsida!
	그래요! 그럼 점심 먹고 바로 홍대로 갑시다!
MinJun:	Sounds good. By the way, I also have an appointment at 7.
	Joayo. Geureonde jega ilgopsiedo yaksogi isseoyo.
	좋아요. 그런데 제가 7시에도 약속이 있어요.
JiYoon:	Then, once the party ends, we can ride the subway over.
	Geureom patiga kkeunnago jihacheoreul tago gamyeon dwaeyo.
	그럼 파티가 끝나고 지하철을 타고 가면 돼요.
MinJun:	Good plan!
	Joayo!
	좋아요!

New Vocabulary 1

breakfast/morning	아침 **achim**
lunch	점심 **jeomsim**
dinner	저녁 **jeonyeok**
subway	지하철 **jihacheol**
party	파티 **pati**
appointment/promise	약속 **yaksok**
directly/straight	바로 **baro**
to end	끝나다 **kkeunnada**
to ride	타다 **tada**
to be correct	맞다 **matda**

GRAMMAR NOTE   Comparing Using 도 *do* "Also"

In Korean, the particle "도" **do** is an essential tool in creating natural and fluid comparisons. 도 **Do** can be translated into English as "also," "as well," or "even though." Let's take a look at some example sentences where 도 **do** is added to nouns to provide additional information.

"제 친구도 왔어요."
Je chingudo wasseoyo.
"My friend also came."

"우리가 점심도 같이 먹었어요."
Uriga jeomsimdo gachi meogeosseoyo.
"We also ate lunch together."

"저도 경기 봤어요!"
Jeodo gyeonggi bwasseoyo!
"I watched the game as well!"

"엄마도 갔어요?"
Eommado gasseoyo?
"Did Mom go as well?"

Anytime you want to include additional information that was not previously mentioned, follow these examples by adding "도" **do** to nouns—this is an effective method.

CULTURAL NOTE Telling Time in Korean

Telling time in Korean is fairly intuitive. In Korean there is the Sino-Korean, or Chinese influenced, number set and the pure Korean number set. When telling time, we use the pure Korean numbers for hours, and Sino-Korean numbers for minutes and seconds.

Here are the number sets:

Sino-Korean	Pure Korean
1. 일 il	하나 hana
2. 이 i	둘 dul
3. 삼 sam	셋 set
4. 사 sa	넷 net
5. 오 o	다섯 daseot
6. 육 yuk	여섯 yeoseot
7. 칠 chil	일곱 ilgop
8. 팔 pal	여덟 yeodeol (ㅂ is silent)
9. 구 gu	아홉 ahop
10. 십 sip	열 yeol

For numbers above ten in Sino-Korean, such as eleven through nineteen, we first state the number ten and then state whatever number follows it. For example, if we want to say fifteen, we would say "ten five" or "십오" **sibo**. Nineteen is "ten nine" or "십구" **sipgu**. This process adds one more step for any numbers between (and including) twenty and ninety-nine. We first state how many tens we have. This means that for the number twenty-three, we have two tens and a three. This results in "two ten three" or "이십삼" **isipsam**. Check out the examples below.

63	⟹	"six ten three" (육십삼 yuksipsam)
87	⟹	"eight ten seven" (팔십칠 palsipchil)
99	⟹	"nine ten nine" (구십구 gusipgu)
44	⟹	"four ten four"(사십사 sasipsa)

The pure Korean number system is more similar to the English number system in which there is a new word for every new ten base. In English, we say ten, twenty, thirty, forty, fifty, etc. Korean has its own base of ten sets as well. Since we are learning about telling time in this chapter, and most clocks only go up to twelve we will stick with learning numbers up to nineteen. The tens placeholder in Korean is simple since it is just the number ten or "열" **yeol**. Easy right? So, we start by saying, "ten" and then add on the pure Korean numbers, one through nine, to make a number above ten. Let's see how this works.

11	⇒	"ten one" (열하나 **yeolhana**)
13	⇒	"ten three" (열셋 **yeolset**)
15	⇒	"ten five" (열다섯 **yeoldaseot**)
17	⇒	"ten seven" (열일곱 **yeolilgop**)

Now that we know the numbers, how do we tell time? Actually, the pure Korean hours change a bit when you tell time. The numbers one through four all lose their last letters when the contracted word for "hour" or "시" **si** is added to them. This is seen in these examples.

1 o'clock	⇒	한시 **hansi** – the "하나" **hana** is contracted to "한" **han**
2 o'clock	⇒	두시 **dusi** – the "ㄹ" is dropped
3 o'clock	⇒	세시 **sesi** – the "ㅅ" is dropped
4 o'clock	⇒	네시 **nesi** – the "ㅅ" is dropped

11 and 12 o'clock then become "열한시" **yeolhansi** and "열두시" **yeoldusi** respectively.

The last things we need to know about telling time are the words:

A.M.	오전	**ojeon**	(오 o meaning "noon" and 전 jeon meaning "before")
P.M.	오후	**ohu**	(오 o meaning "noon" and 후 hu meaning "after")
minute	분	**bun**	
second	초	**cho**	

We then combine all we have learned and say the hour first followed by minutes (and then seconds if necessary).

7:15 AM	⇒	오전 일곱시 십오분 ojeon ilgopsi sibobun
10:45 AM	⇒	오전 열시 사십오분 ojeon yeolsi sasibobun
4:30 PM	⇒	오후 네시 삼십분 ohu nesi samsipbun

Actually, saying 네시 삼십분 **nesi samsipbun** (4:30) is not wrong but most people say 네시 반 **nesi ban**. "반" **Ban** is defined as "half" and is used for expressing "half hour" or the 30 minute mark. So in this case 4:30 would be expressed as 네시 반 **nesi ban** instead of 네시 삼십분 **nesi samsipbun**.

3:00 PM	⇒	오후 세시 ohu sesi
9:57 PM	⇒	오후 아홉시 오십칠분 ohu ahopsi osipchilbun
11:24 AM	⇒	오전 열한시 이십사분 ojeon yeolhansi isipsabun
5:30 PM	⇒	다섯시 반 daseossi ban

Practice Activity 1

Insert the 도 **do** next to the correct noun. Try to put appropriate markers such as 에 **e**, 를 **reul** or 가 **ga** with the other noun.

1. I also want to go to the party.

   나 _____ 파티 _____ 가고 싶어요.

   Na _____ pati _____ gago sipeoyo.

2. My brother also likes baseball (야구).

   나의 형 _____ 야구 _____ 좋아해요.

   Naui hyeong _____ yagu _____ joahaeyo.

3. Even Minjeong did her homework.

   민정이 _____ 숙제 _____ 했어요.

   Minjeongi _____ sukje _____ haesseoyo.

4. My mother likes apples as well.

   저희 엄마 _____ 사과 _____ 좋아해요.

   Jeohui eomma _____ sagwa _____ joahaeyo.

5. The party will be on the 9th as well.

   9일 _____ 파티 _____ 있을 거예요.

   Guil _____ pati _____ isseulgeoyeyo.

🎧 DIALOGUE 2 **Lunch with a Friend**

Sejong and Sehee decide what they want to have for lunch.

Sejong: Today the weather is really good!
          Oneul nalssiga jonne!
          오늘 날씨가 좋네!

Sehee: You're right. Should we go out and get something to eat today?
          Geureone. Geureom oneureun oesigeul halkka?
          그러네. 그럼 오늘은 외식을 할까?

Sejong: Good idea. What should we eat?
          Joa. Mwo meogeulkkka?
          좋아. 뭐 먹을까?

Sehee: I want to eat some pasta, how does that sound?
          Naneun paseutareul meokgo sipeunde, eottae?
          나는 파스타를 먹고 싶은데, 어때?

Sejong: I'm not that into pasta. . . how about we order a pizza?
          Nan paseuta byeolloinde. . . pija sikimyeon eottae?
          난 파스타 별로인데...피자 시키면 어때?

Sehee: Pizza is fine.
          Pija, joa.
          피자, 좋아.

Sejong: Okay, I'll order!
          Geurae, naega jumunhalge!
          그래, 내가 주문할게!

🎧 **New Vocabulary 2**

weather	날씨 **nalssi**
to be good	좋다 **jota**
eating outside	외식 **oesik**
to eat	먹다 **meokda**
to think	생각하다 **saenggakada**
pasta	파스타 **paseuta**
how	어때 **eottae**
(not) particularly	별로 **byeollo**
(별로이다 **byeolloida** = not particularly fond of it)	
pizza	피자 **pija**
to be okay	괜찮다 **gwaenchanta**
to cause something; to order food	시키다 **sikida**
to order food	주문하다 **jumunhada**

GRAMMAR NOTE The Subject Marker

One aspect of Korean that is very different from European languages is that of a subject marker. In most languages we rely on sentence order and context to understand what the subject of the sentence is. While this is mostly true for Korean as well, the subject marker allows the listener to know what the subject is, no matter where it was located in the sentence. In Korean, this marker is represented by 이 **i** or 가 **ga**.

For example, how would we differentiate the sentences, "John eats an apple" and "An apple eats John"? Besides sentence order and the probability of an apple eating someone being microscopically low, we can add 이 **i** or 가 **ga** to the subject to specify who is doing the action of "eating" and what is being acted upon. "John eats an apple" would be represented as: "존이 사과를 먹어요" **Joni sagwareul meogeoyo**. Whereas "An apple eats John" would be: "사과가 존을 먹어요" **Sagwaga joneul meogeoyo**. The 을 **eul**/를 **reul** is an object marker and will be explained later. 이 **I** always attaches to a noun that ends in a consonant while 가 **ga** comes after a noun ending with a vowel. What does this look like? Let's practice.

Ends with a vowel	Ends with a consonant
오늘 날씨가 좋아요. **Oneul nalssiga joayo.** *The weather is good today.*	외식이 편해요. **Oesigi pyeonhaeyo.** *Eating outside is convenient.*
저녁에 파티가 있어요. **Jeonyeoge patiga isseoyo.** *I have a party tonight.*	지하철이 빨라요. **Jihacheori ppallayo.** *Taking the subway is faster.*

Subject and topic markers are two of the most challenging grammar points to learn, in Korean. It will take some time and practice to get used to when to use which, but it might be helpful to remember the guidelines below.

Usually 이 **i** and 가 **ga** put more emphasis on the *subject* of the sentence while 은 **eun** and 는 **neun** put more emphasis on the *action* that occurs in the sentence.

Emphasis on the subject	Emphasis on the action
내가 밥을 먹었다. **Naega babeul meogeotda.** *I had my meal.* (= I am the one who had the meal.)	나는 밥을 먹었다. **Naneun babeul meogeotda.** *I had my meal.*

이 **I** and 가 **ga** are used more with questions and negative sentences when the focus of the sentence is on the subject (as mentioned in Lesson 3).

Focus is on the subject	Less focus is on the subject
존이 한국에 갔어요? **Joni hanguge gasseoyo?** *Did John go to Korea?*	존은 한국에 갔어요? **Joneun hanguge gasseoyo?** *Did John go to Korea?*
제가 안 했어요. **Jega an haesseoyo.** *I didn't do that.* (= I'm not the one who did that.)	저는 안 했어요. **Jeoneun an haesseoyo.** *I didn't do that.*

은 **Eun** and 는 **neun** are used to show a change in the topic of the discussion.

Use of 은 eun	Use of 는 neun
점심은 먹었어? **Jeomsimeun meogeosseo?** *(By the way) Did you have lunch?*	생일파티는 언제야? **Saengilpatineun eonjeya?** *(By the way) When is the birthday party?*

이 **I** and 가 **ga** are used when you mention something for the first time (new information) but 은 **eun** and 는 **neun** are used when you are referring to something you have already talked about (old information).

존이 제 생일 파티에 왔습니다. 존은 큰 선물을 들고 왔습니다. 존은 그 선물을 나에게 주었습니다.
Joni je saengnil patie watseumnida. Joneun keun seonmureul deulgo watseumnida. Joneun geu seonmureul naege jueotseumnida.
John came to my birthday party. He brought a big present. He gave it to me.

CULTURAL NOTE Days of the Week

Days of the week in Korean

Monday	월요일	**woryoil**
Tuesday	화요일	**hwayoil**
Wednesday	수요일	**suyoil**
Thursday	목요일	**mogyoil**
Friday	금요일	**geumyoil**
Saturday	토요일	**toyoil**
Sunday	일요일	**iryoil**

Interestingly, Korean has the same systemology behind choosing these names for the seven-day calendar, as Latin does. Just as Sunday and Monday are named after the Sun and the Moon, the remaining five days were named after the five known planets to the Babylonians, which were named according to famous Norse and Roman gods: Thursday to Thor, Friday to Frigga, the wife of Odin, and Saturday to Saturn, the Roman god of Fun.

It is very important to memorize the days of the week as they are the basis of all dates in Korean. A more fun way to remember the days of the week is by their Sino-Korean meanings that were the original names for the planets.

일 **il**   = 日 (Sun)
월 **wol** = 月 (Moon)
화 **hwa** = 火 (Fire)
수 **su**   = 水 (Water)
목 **mok** = 木 (Tree)
금 **geum** = 金 (Metal)
토 **to**   = 土 (Earth)

Practice Activity 2

Attach 은 **eun**, 는 **neun**, 이 **i** or 가 **ga** to the noun.

1. "MinJeong goes to school."

   "민정이 _____ 학교에 가요."

   Minjeongi _____ hakgyoe gayo.

2. "Sejong likes MinHee."

   "세종 _____ 민희를 좋아해요."

   Sejong _____ minhuireul joahaeyo.

3. "(Today was not fun but) Tomorrow, there will be a fun party."

   "내일 _____ 재미있는 파티를 해요."

   Naeil _____ jaemiinneun patireul haeyo.

4. (The party today was not fun but) Tomorrow, the party will be fun."

   "내일 파티 _____ 재미있을 거예요."

   Naeil pati _____ jaemiisseul geoyeyo.

🎧 ⌜DIALOGUE 3⌟ Saying Goodbye

Somin and Seungwoo say goodbye and plan for another meeting.

Seungwoo: That was fun. When should we meet again?
Jaemiisseosseoyo. Eonje dasi mannalkkayo?
재미있었어요. 언제 다시 만날까요?

Somin: Yeah, it was really fun! Hmm, how about Wednesday?
Ne, jinjja joasseoyo! Eum, suyoireun eottaeyo?
네, 진짜 좋았어요! 음, 수요일은 어때요?

Seungwoo: Wednesday doesn't work, but I have time on Thursday!
Suyoireun andoego mogyoireneun sigani isseoyo!
수요일은 안되고 목요일에는 시간이 있어요!

Somin: Thursday also works. What should we do then?
Mogyoil, joayo. Geuttae uri mwo halkkayo?
목요일, 좋아요. 그때 우리 뭐 할까요?

Seungwoo: I kind of want to eat Italian, how about we go get pasta?
Itaeri eumsik jom meokgo sipeunde, paseuta meogeureo gamyeon eotteolkkayo?
이태리 음식 좀 먹고 싶은데, 파스타 먹으러 가면 어떨까요?

Somin: I also want to eat pasta. How is 5 o'clock?
Nado paseuta meokgo sipeoyo. Daseotsi eottaeyo?
나도 파스타 먹고 싶어요. 5 시 어때요?

Seungwoo: 5 o'clock is good. I'll contact you!
Daseotsi, joayo. Yyeollakalgeyo!
5 시, 좋아요. 연락할게요!

Somin: Okay. See you later!
Geuraeyo. Annyeonghi gaseyo!
그래요. 안녕히 가세요!

🎧 New Vocabulary 3

again	다시	dasi
to meet	만나다	mannada
really	진짜	jinjja
Wednesday	수요일	suyoil
to not be okay	안되다	andoeda
time	때	ttae
what	뭐	mwo
Thursday	목요일	mogyoil
time	시간	sigan

Italian	이태리 itaeri
again/also	또 tto
to contact	연락하다 yeollakada
peacefully	안녕히 annyeonghi

GRAMMAR NOTE The Polite Ending

As we briefly mentioned earlier, the polite ending is the most commonly used verb ending in the Korean language. The polite form can be used by anyone and spoken to almost anyone. Understanding this ending is an essential part to becoming proficient in Korean and is the foundation for many other grammar forms and endings.

To conjugate a verb into the polite ending, you remove the 다 da at the end of every verb (가다 gada, to go; 먹다 meokda, to eat; 괜찮다 gwaenchanta, to be ok, etc.). After you remove the 다 da, if the last vowel is an ㅏ a or ㅗ o then an 아 a is added in place of the 다 da. If the final vowel is an ㅜ u, ㅓ eo, -eu, or ㅣ i then an 어 eo is added in place of the 다 da. If the final vowel is already an ㅏ a or ㅓ eo then you may contract and an extra ㅏ a or ㅓ eo is not needed. If the final vowel is an ㅗ o or ㅜ u then they can be combined with ㅏ a or ㅓ eo to create the diphthongs ㅘ wa and ㅝ wo. Some examples:

	Basic Form		To Conjugate Polite Form Verbs			
to live	살다 salda	살 sal	⟹	살아 sara		
to eat	먹다 meokda	먹 meok	⟹	먹어 meogeo		
to go	가다 gada	가 ga	⟹	가아 gaa	⟹	가 ga
to stand	서다 seoda	서 seo	⟹	서어 seoeo	⟹	서 seo
to come	오다 oda	오 o	⟹	오아 oa	⟹	와 wa
to give	주다 juda	주 ju	⟹	주어 jueo	⟹	줘 jwo

Although we won't go into much detail here, it's important to know that some verbs and adjectives have irregular inflections. For example, if the last consonant is a ㅂ b then the ㅂ b is eliminated and an 우 u or 오 o is added. The normal conjugation of 우다 uda or 오다 oda is then followed. A good example of this conjugation is the verb 눕다 nupda (to lay down) and the adjective 곱다 gopda (pretty), respectively.

눕다 nupda	눕 nup	누 nu	누우 nuu	누우어 nuueo	누워 nuwo
곱다 gopda	곱 gop	고 go	고오 goo	고오아 gooa	고와 gowa

Lastly, to complete the conjugation, add the polite word ending 요 yo. It looks like this:

BASIC	POLITE (+ yo)
먹어 **meogeo** (to eat)	먹어요 **meogeoyo**
가 **ga** (to go)	가요 **gayo**
와 **wa** (to come)	와요 **wayo**
누워 **nuwo** (to lie)	누워요 **nuwoyo**

Using the polite form will make a great first impression with whoever you talk to and will create a good foundation of respect.

CULTURAL NOTE   Different Ways to Leave a Meeting

The words and gestures you use before departing from any kind of meeting will leave a lasting impression and can greatly enhance a relationship. Here are phrases that work in almost any setting when leaving a meeting.

Stay peacefully (used when you are the one leaving)
안녕히 계세요 **Annyeonghi gyeseyo**

Go peacefully (used when you are staying)
안녕히 가세요 **Annyeonghi gaseyo**

Stay healthy 건강하세요 **Geonganghaseyo**

Go carefully 조심히 가세요 **Josimhi gaseyo**

See you again (used informally with friends)
또 봐요 **Tto bwayo**

Using these common phrases, with a slight bow or handshake, will definitely impress and help you maintain good relationships with those you meet.

Practice Activity 3

Conjugate the following verbs using the polite ending and add them to their corresponding sentences.

come down/descend	내리다	**naerida**
to go	가다	**gada**
to eat	먹다	**meokda**
to close (eyes)	감다	**gamda**
to ride	타다	**tada**

1. Minji _____ apples.

   민지가 사과를 _____.

   Minjiga sagwareul _____.

2. Unyoung _____ bikes.

   운영이 자전거를 _____.

   Unyeongi jajeongeoreul _____.

3. Jiyoon _____ to school.

   지윤이가 학교에 _____.

   Jiyuniga hakgyoe _____.

4. Cheolsoo _____ his eyes.

   철수가 눈을 _____.

   Cheolsuga nuneul _____.

5. Rain _____ from the sky.

   하늘에서 비가 _____.

   Haneureseo biga _____.

Oh, I know this person. She is my senior.

Eo! Naega aneun saramine. I saram uri hakgyo seonbaeya.

Really? She is my older sister.

Eo? I saram uri nunaya.

Oh. Is she?

A jeongmal?

Yes. She is very kind. Let's study together at my house. You'll be able to meet her.

Eung. Aju chakae. Uri jibeseo gachi gongbuhaja. Nunareul mannal su isseul geoya.

Okay. How many siblings do you have?

Geurae. Neo hyeongjega myeon myeongiya?

I have an older brother, a younger brother, and a younger sister.

Hyeongi han myeong deo itgo, namdongsaengi han myeong, yeodongsaengi han myeong isseo.

LESSON 5
Talking About Family and Home

🎧 ⸬DIALOGUE 1⸬ **My Brothers and Sisters**

Mansu and Mina look at pictures on a phone together and discover they have a common acquaintance.

Mina: (*looking at a selfie on Mansu's phone*) Oh, I know this person. She is my senior.
Eo! Naega aneun saramine. I saram uri hakgyo seonbaeya.
어! 내가 아는 사람이네. 이 사람 우리 학교 선배야.

Mansu: Really? She is my older sister.
Eo? I saram uri nunaya.
어? 이 사람 우리 누나야.

Mina: Oh. Is she?
A jeongmal?
아 정말?

Mansu: Yes. She is very kind. Let's study together at my house. You'll be able to meet her.
Eung. Aju chakae. Uri jibeseo gachi gongbuhaja. Nunareul mannal su isseul geoya.
응. 아주 착해. 우리 집에서 같이 공부하자. 누나를 만날 수 있을 거야.

Mina: Okay. How many siblings do you have?
Geurae. Neo hyeongjega myeon myeongiya?
그래. 너 형제가 몇 명이야?

Mansu: I have an older brother, a younger brother, and a younger sister.
Hyeongi han myeong deo itgo, namdongsaengi han myeong, yeodongsaengi han myeong isseo.
형이 한 명 더 있고, 남동생이 한 명, 여동생이 한 명 있어.

🎧 **New Vocabulary 1**

senior	선배	seonbae
older sister of a male	누나	nuna
siblings	형제	hyeongje
how many	몇	myeot
younger sibling	동생	dongsaeng
older brother of a male	형	hyeong
younger brother	남동생	namdongsaeng
younger sister	여동생	yeodongsaeng

GRAMMAR NOTE   Verbs and Adjectives

In Lesson 1, you learned that Korean sentences end with verbs. You may have also encountered some sentences ending with words which, when translated into English, would be adjectives. This is because, in Korean, 똑똑하다 **ttokttokada** (to be smart) functions as a verb just like 생각하다 **saenggakada** (to think). It may be helpful to think of these as descriptive verbs and action verbs.

Because the distinction between English verbs and adjectives almost entirely disappears in Korean, some sentences should be translated in a less literal way, using whichever part of speech seems natural. For example, 좋다 **jota** means "good," and is a descriptive verb; however, you should translate the sentence "저는 한식이 좋아요" **Jeoneun hansigi joayo** (literally, "To me, Korean food is good") as in "I like Korean food –" using the verb "to like" instead of the adjective "good."

Sometimes this causes confusion. To make sure you understand the idea behind a Korean sentence, pay attention to the markers in a sentence (which you learned in Lesson 4). For example, 무섭다 **museopda** (scary) is a descriptive verb that is often misused. The sentence "저는 사자가 무서워요" **Jeoneun sajaga museowoyo**, in which the speaker is the topic and lions are the subject, means "To me, lions are scary," or, better yet, "I am scared of lions."

You can also conjugate Korean verb stems into modifiers. This section will show you how to do so in the present tense. To make adjectives out of descriptive verbs, drop the verb's ending. Look at the last letter in the verb stem. If it is a vowel, add -ㄴ **n**. If it is a consonant, add -은 **eun**. For example:

똑똑하다 ttokttokada ⮕ 똑똑하 ttokttoka ⮕ 똑똑한 사람 ttokttokan saram
(a smart person)

작다 jakda ⮕ 작 jak ⮕ 작은 책 jageun chaek
(a small book)

You can make present participles out of action verbs. To do so, drop the verb's ending and add -는 **neun** (regardless of the verb stem's ending). For example:

웃다 utda ⮕ 웃 ut ⮕ 웃는 학생 unneun haksaeng
(the student who is laughing)

가다 gada ⮕ 가 ga ⮕ 가는 사람 ganeun saram
(the person who is going)

있다 **Itda**/없다 **eopda** (to exist/not to exist) follow rules of action verbs when being conjugated. Therefore, 맛 있다 **mat itda** (to be delicious) becomes 맛 있는 **mat inneun** (delicious).

Some verbs are irregular, and their stems will have to be modified before they can become adjectives or participles. When conjugating ㅂ **b-** irregular verbs, which have stems ending with -ㅂ **b**, drop the -ㅂ **b** and substitute with -우 **u**. The rest of the steps are the same. 춥다 **Chupda** (to be cold) would be modified as follows:

춥다 **chupda** ⟶ 춥 **chup** ⟶ 추 **chu** ⟶ 추우 **chuu** ⟶ 추운 **chuun**

ㄹ **r**-irregular verbs have stems that end in -ㄹ **r**. These verbs are simple. When conjugating, drop the -ㄹ **r** (and don't add anything else before the modifier's ending). Therefore, 만들다 **mandeulda** (to make) is modified this way:

만들다 **mandeulda** ⟶ 만들 **mandeul** ⟶ 만드 **mandeu** ⟶ 만드는 **mandeuneun**

You will learn more about irregular verbs as you continue your studies of Korean.

CULTURAL NOTE   Sibling Terms and Respect

Korea is a traditionally Confucian society, so relationships are clearly defined and hierarchical. Different roles carry different behavioral expectations, for example, 선배 **seonbae** are students or employees who are senior to but do not have authority over others, and 후배 **hubae** are their junior counterparts.

Traditionally, 선배 **seonbae** and 후배 **hubae** help each other in different ways. For example, 후배 **hubae** are expected to defer to the wisdom of their 선배 **sonbae** or help them by carrying their things. 선배 **Seonbae** are supposed to buy meals or other things for their 후배 **hubae**. However, with the fast-changing cultural norms, Korea today has a mixture of this traditional social role and social behaviors based on individualism.

To interact appropriately with Koreans, be sure to consider age, grade level, and the social status of those who you are interacting with.

Sibling terms are another way to define relationships and show respect even for those outside of your actual family members. Sibling terms feel more intimate than 선배 **sonbae** and 후배 **hubae** do, so juniors should wait for seniors to invite them to use those terms. The invitation will be obvious. If you are a woman, you may meet someone, realize she is a year or two older than you, and watch her eyes light up as she says, "You can call me **eonni** (언니 older sister)!" If you are a man, you may meet an older male who thinks of you as 동생 **dongsaeng** (younger brother) and calls you by your first name without any following terms or titles, in which case you may call him 형 **hyeong** (older brother).

Other filial terms are employed in a variety of community interactions. You may inquire after an elderly lady's health by calling her 할머니 **halmeoni** (grandmother), whether you've ever met her before or not.

You can call a grown man 아저씨 **ajeossi** (uncle) regardless of his social status. This term does not imply politeness nor inhospitality. 아줌마 **Ajumma**, (aunt,) used to be just as appropriate for women as 아저씨 **ajeossi** is for men, but now has a negative connotation. Thus, sometimes 이모 **imo** (your mother's sister) is used for calling a middle-aged waitress, for example. Keep in mind that middle-aged Korean women, like middle-aged women in many other cultures, may be sensitive about their ages. When you refer to a woman whose age is similar to or less than yours, 아가씨 **agassi** (sister, miss) is appropriate. However, it is regarded offensive when you call a middle-aged or older woman 아가씨 **agassi**.

There are exceptions, changes to usage norms, and other cultural nuances foreigners may find surprising. Some are made in an effort to be professional: customer service employees may (or may not) speak to you as if you were older than them even if you are not. Other changes are becoming popular among younger Koreans who wish to minimize traditional, gendered power dynamics. Some female college students refer to male seniors as 형 **hyeong**. Some sons-in-law are using more respectful terms for their parents-in-law than was historically common.

Practice Activity 1

Match the following verbs and adjectives with the appropriate conjugation form.

1. 괜찮다 **gwaenchanta** (to be okay/fine) _____   a. 좋은

2. 있다 **itda** (to exist) _____   b. 괜찮은

3. 없다 **eopda** (to not exist) _____   c. 없는

4. 쉽다 **swipda** (easy) _____   d. 아는

5. 중요하다 **jungyohada** (important) _____   e. 중요한

6. 알다 **alda** (to know) _____   f. 쉬운

7. 좋다 **jota** (to be good) _____   g. 있는

Practice Activity 2

Make the phrase by conjugating the action verb or descriptive verb into adjectives or present participles.

Example:
맛있다 **masitda**, 한식 **hansik** = 맛있는 한식 **masinneun hansik**
(delicious Korean food)

1. 오다 **oda** (to come, road),

   길 **gil** = _____

2. 주문하다 **jumunhada** (to order food, pasta),

   파스타 **paseuta** = _____

3. 중요하다 **jungyohada** (important, test),

   시험 **siheom** = _____

4. 반갑다 **bangapda** ([to be] nice to meet, friend),

   친구 **chingu** = _____

5. 재미있다 **jaemiitda** (interesting, movie),

   영화 **yeonghwa** = _____

Practice Activity 3

Fill in the blanks with their proper meaning in English or Korean.

1. younger brother _____

2. 여동생 **yeodongsaeng** _____

3. senior _____

4. how many _____

5. 형 **hyeong** _____

6. 누나 **nuna** _____

 **DIALOGUE 2 : In My House**

Mina learns social etiquette for entering a home at Mansu's house.

Mansu: This is our home! Come on in.
    Yeogiga uri jibiya. Deureowa.
    여기가 우리 집이야. 들어와.

Mina: Great! Thanks for inviting me.
    Eung. Chodaehae jwoseo gomawo.
    응. 초대해 줘서 고마워.

Mansu: No problem. Oh, and just so you know, we take shoes off in our
    house.
    Aniya. Cham, urineun jip aneseo sinbareul beoseo.
    아니야. 참, 우리는 집 안에서 신발을 벗어.

Mina: Oh, okay. Where should I leave my shoes?
    A, algesseo. Sinbareun eodie dulkka?
    아, 알겠어. 신발은 어디에 둘까?

Mansu: You can just leave them by the door. We don't have a shoe closet.
    Geunyang mun yeope dwo. Urineun sinbaljangi eopseo.
    그냥 문 옆에 둬. 우리는 신발장이 없어.

Mina: Okay. Oh? The floor is warm. I like it.
    Arasseo. Badagi ttatteutane. Jota.
    알았어. 바닥이 따뜻하네. 좋다.

Mansu: Yes. In Korea, underfloor heating is popular.
    Eung. Hangugeseoneun ondollo nanbangeul hae.
    응. 한국에서는 온돌로 난방을 해.

🎧 New Vocabulary 2

home	집 **jip**
come in	들어오다 **deureooda**
to invite	초대하다 **chodaehada**
you're welcome (basic meaning is "no.")	아니다 **anida**
shoes	신발 **sinbal**
to take off	벗다 **beotda**
to leave, to put	두다 **duda**
I see	알겠다 **algetda**
door	문 **mun**
next to	옆 **yeop**
shoe closet	신발장 **sinbaljang**
to not exist	없다 **eopda**
floor	바닥 **badak**
to be warm	따뜻하다 **ttatteutada**
underfloor heating system	온돌 **ondol**
heating	난방 **nanbang**

GRAMMAR NOTE Possession

One of the more commonly used grammar forms in Korean is the expression of possession or lack of possession. A typical English sentence looks like, "I have a book" or "Susan doesn't have a house." It is most often formed by starting with the noun that one possesses or does not possess (a book or a house), then adding the subject marker that we learned in Lesson 4, 이 **i**/가 **ga**, and then using the ending 있다 **itda** (to exist) or 없다 **eopda** (to not exist). Once you put all the parts together and conjugate the ending it will look like:

책이 있어요. **Chaegi isseoyo.** *I have a book.*
수잔은 집이 없어요. **Sujaneun jibi eopseoyo.** *Susan doesn't have a house.*

Often in speech or when the item that is possessed is clearly understood, the 이 **i**/가 **ga** can be dropped from the sentence. We will learn more about dropping markers in Lesson 6.

CULTURAL NOTE Wearing Shoes

In Korea (and other parts of Asia), wearing shoes indoors has long since been considered unacceptable. Historically, and presently, in some areas of Korea, traditional homes called **hanok** (한옥) were equipped with **ondol** (온돌), an underfloor heating system. Residents and guests alike would leave their shoes on the ground when they stepped up off the dusty road. For a culture that dined on cushions and unfolded sleeping mats onto the floors, it was especially important to keep things clean. Traditionally, homeowners would encourage guests to sit or sleep on the warmest spot on the floor. In older, countryside houses, this is still the tradition.

Modern homes are somewhat different than **hanok** and often have entry-ways (현관 **hyeongwan**) which require guests to step up into the rest of the home. As a guest, you should leave your shoes with the other shoes, piled by the door or resting on a small set of steps, and keep your socks on. Some businesses also require you to remove your shoes, but will provide "slippers" (슬리퍼 **seullipeo**, slides for wearing inside). For example, you may sit sock-footed in a restaurant, but borrow a pair of plastic sandals lying inside its restroom. Some places have lockers for your shoes, but you may take comfort in Korea's low crime rates. Slippers are worn at some schools (not universities) and workplaces. Other places don't expect you to take your shoes off. If the place is more traditional or more homey, it is more likely someone may ask you to remove your shoes, but the best way to know what is expected of you is to glance at the locals inside.

Practice Activity 4

Match Korean words with the appropriate English translations.

1. 집 **jip** _____   a. not exist

2. 신발 **sinbal** _____   b. shoes

3. 초대하다 **chodaehada** _____   c. home

4. 신발장 **sinbaljang** _____   d. to invite

5. 온돌 **ondol** _____   e. shoe closet

6. 없다 **eopda** _____   f. underfloor heating system

Practice Activity 5

Circle the correct particle (이 **i**/ 가 **ga**) and expression of possession (있어요 **isseoyo**/ 없어요 **eopseoyo**) in each sentence.

1. I have a younger brother. (**namdongsaeng**)

    남동생 (이 / 가) (있어요 / 없어요).

2. I don't have a charger. (**chungjeongi**)

    충전기 (이 / 가) (있어요 / 없어요).

3. I have a shoe closet. (**sinbaljang**)

    신발장 (이 / 가) (있어요 / 없어요).

4. I have a hair straightener. (**godegi**)

    고데기 (이 / 가) (있어요 / 없어요).

5. I don't have a wallet. (**jigap**)

    지갑 (이 / 가) (있어요 / 없어요).

Practice Activity 6

Translate the English sentences into Korean. In Korean you do not need to include yourself in the sentence. We assume it is about you.

Example:
여동생이 있어요.
Yeodongsaengi isseoyo.
I have a younger sister.

(Remember that in speech you can drop the subject and topic marker. It looks like 여동생 있어요 **yeodongsaeng isseoyo.**)

1. I don't have a younger brother. _____

2. I have a friend. _____

3. I don't have time. _____

4. I have a bag. _____

5. I don't have shoes. _____

🎧 ┊DIALOGUE 3┊ **My Parents**

Mina meets Minsu's parents and grandmother.

Mom: Mansu! Is this your friend?
       Mansuya, ne chinguni?
       만수야, 네 친구니?

Mansu: Yes, mom. This is my friend Mina. Mina, these are my parents.
       Ne, eomma. I chinguga minayeyo. Minaya, uri bumonimiya.
       네, 엄마. 이 친구가 민아예요. 민아야, 우리 부모님이야.

Mina:	(bowing) Mr. and Mrs. Kim, I'm pleased to meet you! **(insa) eomeonim, abeonim, annyeonghaseyo!** (인사) 어머님, 아버님, 안녕하세요!
Mr. and Mrs. Kim:	We're pleased [to meet you too]! **Geurae bangapda!** 그래 반갑다!
Dad:	Mansu, make sure to greet your grandma! She is in the living room. **Mansuya, halmeonihantedo insa deuryeora. Geosire gyesida.** 만수야, 할머니한테도 인사 드려라. 거실에 계시다.
Mansu:	Yes, I will. **Ne, geureolgeyo.** 네, 그럴게요.

🎧 **New Vocabulary 3**

mom, mommy	엄마 **eomma**
mother	어머니 **eomeoni** (어머님 **eomeonim**)
dad, daddy	아빠 **appa**
father	아버지 **abeoji** (아버님 **abeonim**)
parents	부모 **bumo** (부모님 **bumonim**)
grandmother	할머니 **halmeoni** (할머님 **halmeonim**)
to give greetings (honorific form)	인사 드리다 **insa deurida**
living room/family room	거실 **geosil**
to exist (honorific form)	계시다 **gyesida**
I will do it in that way.	그럴게요 **geureolgeyo** (그렇게 할게요 **geureoke halgeyo**)

GRAMMAR NOTE **Honorific Endings**

Honorific suffixes are another way to verbalize respect. -씨 **Ssi** is the most versatile, equivalent to "Mr.," "Ms.," or "Mrs."; it can be attached to a given (personal) name, a family name, or a full name.

-님 **Nim** is even more respectful than -씨 **ssi**. You have already seen it in the word 선생님 **seonsaengnim**. -님 **Nim**, unlike -씨 **ssi**, is more likely to be placed after a person's role than their name. 부처님 **Bucheonim** (Buddha, buddha + -님 **nim**) and 하나님 **hananim** (God, in monotheistic traditions—"one" + -님 **nim**) are often-used examples. -님 **Nim** can also come after professional titles, such as 대표님 **daepyonim** (which literally means "representative," but refers to the president of an organization—equivalent to the English "CEO") and 팀장님 **timjangnim** (team leader); military rank; and filial terms. When -님 **nim** is used with both a name and a title, the name comes first, and the title and suffix follow (e.g. 배 팀장님 **bae timjangnim**, 김상호 대표님 **gimsangho daepyonim**).

Generally, people who are close to and/or younger than the speaker go by their first name without honorifics. However, there are also honorific suffixes for those who are younger than the speaker. Nowadays, they are used infrequently, and almost exclusively in formal situations (e.g. between wedding guests). -양 **Yang** can be added to a young female's name, and -군 **gun** is for young males. The other honorific suffixes can also be attached to titles indicating a lower relationship, while still showing respect to your listener, e.g. 따님 **ttanim** for your boss' daughter and 아드님 **adeunim** for your boss' son.

CULTURAL NOTE   Honoring Parents and Grandparents

In Korea, it is important to show respect to your elders. Some methods for demonstrating respect are by your word choice. You have already learned about different levels of politeness in speech. Some families use honorifics at home, and others do not; most Koreans would use them, at least, when speaking to others about their elders. You can also use honorific words (e.g. using 계시다 **gyesida** in place of 있다 **itda**), which you will learn about later.

Koreans will also demonstrate respect for parents and grandparents through their actions. Day-to-day, they will be deferential and may ask for advice. They try to ease the burdens of those with older bodies—for example, by giving up a train seat. When greeting each other, young people bow first, and more deeply.

Lifestyles are influenced by respect for one's elders. For example, parents closely supervise and guide their children's education and career preparation, so most young Koreans would feel uncomfortable pursuing a career their parents did not approve of.

Respect is also ritualized. For example, the lunar new year is celebrated with deep bows from younger to older generations. Koreans bow first to the oldest generation present, and then to the next oldest (i.e. to grandparents before parents). After bowing, they receive advice and encouragement (and an envelope full of money). Historically, this process begins with a deep bow to deceased ancestors. Although that part of lunar new year as well as providing food for ancestors is getting less popular.

Practice Activity 7

Match the informal words with their polite version.

1. 엄마 **eomma** _____
2. 아빠 **appa** _____
3. 부모 **bumo** _____
4. 할머니 **halmeoni** _____

a. 아버지 **abeoji**

b. 할머님 **halmeonim**

c. 어머니 **eomeoni**

d. 부모님 **bumonim**

e. 아버님 **abeonim**

f. 어머님 **eomeonim**

Practice Activity 8

Match the Korean words with the appropriate English translations.

1. 그럴게요 **geureolgeyo** _____
2. 거실 **geosil** _____
3. 인사 드리다 **insa deurida** _____
4. 부모 **bumo** _____
5. 계시다 **gyesida** _____
6. 할머니 **halmeoni** _____

a. grandmother

b. I will do it in that way

c. parents

d. to exist (honorific form)

e. living room/family room

f. to greet (honorific form)

Practice Activity 9

Circle the proper honorific term of address, if applicable, for each person.

1. Your grandmother 할머니씨 / 할머님

2. Your section chief 부장군 / 부장님

3. Professor Lee 이 교수님 / 이 교수

4. Your team leader 팀장님 / 팀장양

5. Younger brother 남동생님 / 남동생

Hello, how can I help you?
Annyeonghaseyo gogaengnim, eotteoke dowa deurilkkayo?

How can I get to Seoul Station?
Seoulyeokkkaji eotteoke ganayo?

The quickest way is to take the Airport Railroad.
Gonghangcheoldoro gasimyeon jeil ppallayo

Okay. Where can I ride the Airport Railroad?
Gonghangcheoldoneun eodieseo tal su isseoyo?

It's underground.
Jihacheungeseo tasil su itseumnida.

LESSON 6
Asking Directions and Locations

🎧 ⦂DIALOGUE 1⦂ **From the Airport to Seoul**

Sarah asks a passerby how to get to Seoul Station.

Ayoung: Hello, how can I help you?
Annyeonghaseyo gogaengnim, eotteoke dowa deurilkkayo?
안녕하세요 고객님, 어떻게 도와 드릴까요?

Sarah: How can I get to Seoul Station?
Seoulyeokkkaji eotteoke ganayo?
서울역까지 어떻게 가나요?

Ayoung: The quickest way is to take the Airport Railroad.
Gonghangcheoldoro gasimyeon jeil ppallayo.
공항철도로 가시면 제일 빨라요.

Sarah: Okay. Where can I ride the Airport Railroad?
Gonghangcheoldoneun eodieseo tal su isseoyo?
공항철도는 어디에서 탈 수 있어요?

Ayoung: It's underground.
Jihacheungeseo tasil su itseumnida.
지하층에서 타실 수 있습니다.

🎧 **New Vocabulary 1**

customer	고객님 **gogaengnim** (님 **nim** is an honorific suffix)
Seoul Station	서울역 **seoulyeok**
up to a certain point	까지 **kkaji**
Airport Railroad	공항철도 **gonghangcheoldo**
to be quick	빠르다 **ppareuda**
underground or basement	지하층 **jihacheung**
to help	돕다 **dopda**
how	어떻게 **eotteoke**

GRAMMAR NOTE **Locative Markers**

As we have previously learned, Korean uses markers to denote topic (은 **eun** / 는 **neun**), subject (이 **i** / 가 **ga**) and object (을 **eul** / 를 **reul**). Korean also uses markers to denote location and direction. We will look at some basic markers for location in this lesson.

Note: You can use these markers in other contexts as will be discussed in Lesson 7, but for now we will focus on how they are used to denote location.

에 *e* at, to

We use 에 **e** to mark where *something exists or a direction of travel*. We cannot express what is happening at a location using 에 **e**—merely the static location. Let's look at some examples:

철수 씨가 어디에 있어요?
Cheolsu ssiga eodie isseoyo?
Where is Chulsu?

We are asking where Chulsu is so we use 에 **e**.

사라 씨는 학교에 있어요.
Sara ssineun hakgyoe isseoyo
Sarah is at school.

Sarah is at school, but we don't know what she's doing.

서울역은 서울에 있어요.
Seoulyeogeun seoure isseoyo.
The Seoul Station is in Seoul.

에서 *eseo* at, from

We use 에서 **eseo** to mark the *location of an action or simply to state where something is from*. Let's look at some examples:

철수 씨가 한국에서 왔어요
Cheolsu ssiga hangugeseo wasseoyo.
Chulsu came from Korea.

This means that Chulsu is from Korea so we use 에서 **eseo**. If we used 에 **e** here it would mean that Chulsu came to Korea.

사라 씨는 학교에서 공부해요
Sara ssineun hakgyoeseo gongbuhaeyo.
Sarah is studying at school.

This means that the location of the action (Sara's studying) is at the school so we would need to use 에서 **eseo** to show action.

(으) 로 *euro* in the direction of, towards

This marker is used to denote the direction of travel. It can be used with present progressive conjugations, "-고 있다" **go itda**. Let's look at some examples:

철수 씨는 집으로 가고 있어요
Cheolsu ssineun jibeuro gago isseoyo
Chulsu is going home.

사라 씨는 학교로 가고 있어요
Sarassineun hakgyoro gago isseoyo
Sarah is going to school.

Both of these show the direction Chulsu and Sarah are going but don't indicate what they are doing or where they are right now.

이쪽으로 오세요
ijjogeuro oseyo
Please come here.

In this sentence the speaker is not asking the listener to come to a specific location, so using 으로 **euro** here best denotes a vague direction the speaker is asking the listener to come to. It means "Come in this direction" or "Come this way." This is a common phrase in Korea.

까지 *kkaji* up to a point

까지 **Kkaji** is used in a number of ways. The examples below show how to ask directions when describing the starting point and the end point. Let's look at some examples:

서울역까지 얼마나 걸려요?
Seoulyeokkkaji eolmana geollyeoyo?
How long does it take to get to Seoul Station?

The Seoul Station is a fixed location we are trying to get to. Because we are referring to an action we cannot use 에 **e** in this context, so we have to use another marker, in this case, 까지 **kkaji**.

승우 씨의 집에서 학교까지 어떻게 가요?
Seungu ssiui jibeseo hakgyokkaji eotteoke gayo?
How do I get from Seungwoo's house to school?

So, when we ask how to get from one location to another, we need to use 에서 **eseo** (meaning "from") and 까지 **kkaji** (meaning "to") to denote the starting and ending points. Leaving these markers out would result in a very vague and confusing question.

CULTURAL NOTE **Things to Know about Incheon Airport**

If you are traveling to Korea you are probably going to be traveling through Incheon (인천 **Incheon**) International Airport. This is located just west of Seoul and also provides a number of domestic routes for those looking to get out of the city and explore some of Korea's natural beauty. The best way to get from the airport to Seoul is the Airport Railroad (공항철도 **gonghangcheol-do**). This subway line provides direct access to Seoul Station as well as other locations in central Seoul including Hongdae (홍대 **Hongdae**). The Airport Railroad also offers connections to most of the other subway lines that run in and out of Seoul. Also, when you leave Korea from Incheon Airport, be sure to check out the cultural exhibits they have around the airport. Often, there are performances with traditional Korean instruments and chances to show off your Korean writing.

Practice Activity 1

Match the Korean words with the appropriate English translations.

1. 에 **e** _____

2. 에서 **eseo** _____

a. at, from

b. a customer

3. 고객 **gogaek** _____   c. how

4. 빠르다 **ppareuda** _____   d. at, to

5. 어떻게 **eotteoke** _____   e. to be quick

6. 까지 **kkaji** _____   f. up to a certain point

Practice Activity 2

Circle the proper particle (에 **e** / 에서 **eseo**).

1. Sarah came from Spain.
   사라는 스페인   (에 / 에서)   왔어요.

   Saraneun Seupein _____ **wasseoyo.**

2. I'm home.
   저는 집   (에 / 에서)   있어요.

   Jeoneun jib _____ **isseoyo.**

3. Seungwoo, where is your class?
   승우 씨, 수업이 어디   (에 / 에서)   있어요?

   Seungu ssi, sueobi eodi _____ **isseoyo?**

4. Where did Subom come from?
   수범 씨는 어디   (에 / 에서)   왔어요?

   Subeom ssineun eodi _____ **wasseoyo?**

5. Minyoung, where are you?
   민영 씨, 어디   (에 / 에서)   있어요?

   Minyeong ssi, eodi _____ **isseoyo?**

Practice Activity 3

Write the appropriate locative marker (에 **e**, 에서 **eseo**, (으)로 **(eu)ro**, 까지 **kkaji**) in the blanks.

1. 공항 _____ 부산 _____ 얼마나 걸려요?

   Gonghang _____ **Busan** _____ **eolmana geollyeoyo?**

   How long does it take from the airport to Busan?

2. 철수 씨, 공항____ 뭐 해요?

   Cheolsu ssi gonghang _____ mwo haeyo?

   Chulsu, what are you doing at the airport?

3. 민기 씨는 어디 _____ 있어요?

   Mingi ssineun eodi _____ isseoyo?

   Where is Mingi?

4. 롯데 월드 _____ 얼마나 걸려요?

   Rotde woldeu _____ eolmana geollyeoyo?

   How long does it take to get to Lotte World?

5. 저는 서울역 _____ 가고 있어요.

   Jeoneun Seoulyeok _____ gago isseoyo.

   I am going to Seoul Station.

6. 고객님, 이쪽 _____ 오세요.

   Gogaengnim, ijjok _____ oseyo.

   Please come here.

🎧 ┆ DIALOGUE 2 ┆ Getting Around Seoul

Maria plans to go to Korea and asks Seungwoo how to get around Seoul.

Maria:	Seungwoo, have you been to Seoul? **Seungu ssi, hoksi Seoure ga bwasseoyo?** 승우 씨, 혹시 서울에 가 봤어요?
Seungwoo:	Yes, I have been to Seoul. **Ne. Seoure ga bwasseoyo** 네. 서울에 가 봤어요.
Maria:	I'm going to Seoul next month. Which transportation system should I use? **Jega daeumdare seoure gayo. Seoureseo eotteon gyotong sudaneul iyonghaeya haeyo?** 제가 다음달에 서울에 가요. 서울에서 어떤 교통 수단을 이용해야 해요?
Seungwoo:	The bus or the subway is the best. **Beoseuna jihacheori gajang joayo.** 버스나 지하철이 가장 좋아요.

Maria: Thank you, Seungwoo!!
            Ne. Gamsahamnida, seungu ssi!!
            네. 감사합니다, 승우 씨!!

🎧 **New Vocabulary 2**

next month	다음달	**daeumdal**
transportation	교통	**gyotong**
means, method	수단	**sudan**
use, utilize	이용하다	**iyonghada**
bus	버스	**beoseu**
taxi	택시	**taeksi**

GRAMMAR NOTE **The Object Marker 을/를**

As we mentioned in Lesson three, objects within a sentence are denoted using the object markers 을 **eul** for words ending in consonants and 를 **reul** for words ending in vowels.

Examples:
밥 **bab** rice   ➡   밥을 **babeul**
차 **cha** tea   ➡   차를 **chareul**

Let's look at an example sentence.
      지호가 차를 마신다.
      Jihoga chareul masinda.
      Jiho drinks tea.

First, remember that Jiho is the subject and his name takes the subject marker 가 **ga**, which we already learned about.

Tea is the object and takes the object marker 를 **reul**.

Let's look at some more example sentences.
      캐서린이 밥을 먹는다.
      Kaeseorini babeul meongneunda.
      Catherine is eating.

      승우가 버스를 탄다.
      Seunguga beoseureul tanda.
      Seungwoo takes the bus.

CULTURAL NOTE Stopping Someone to Ask for Help

Koreans normally keep to themselves when they are in a public setting, but they are more than willing to help you if you ask. When you ask someone for help, you should be polite and use honorifics. As we have discussed, a great way to get someone's attention is by saying 저기요 **jeogiyo** which is just like saying "Excuse me" in English. Then follow that by saying 죄송한데 혹시 **Joesonghande hoksi**. What we are saying here is, "Sorry to bother you, but do you happen to… ." Let's look at the examples below:

If I needed help finding the nearest bathroom I could say to a passerby:

저기요! 죄송한데 혹시 화장실이 어디 있는지 아세요?
Jeogiyo! Joesonghande hoksi hwajangsiri eodi inneunji aseyo?
Excuse me! Sorry to bother you, but do you happen to know where the bathroom is?

Or another example:

저기요! 죄송한데 어떤 버스를 타야 서울역까지 갈 수 있어요?
Jeogiyo! Joesonghande eotteon beoseureul taya seoulyeokkkaji gal su isseoyo?
Excuse me! Sorry to ask, but what bus should I take to get to Seoul Station?

Practice Activity 4

Translate each English word into Korean.

1. next month   _____

2. transportation   _____

3. method   _____

4. use, utilize   _____

5. bus   _____

6. taxi   _____

Practice Activity 5

Decide which object marker (을 **eul** /를 **reul**) is appropriate for each sentence.

1. 저는 그 사람 _____ 좋아해요.

   Jeoneun geu saram _____ joahaeyo.

   I like that person.

2. 제가 김치 _____ 좋아해요.

    Jega gimchi _____ joahaeyo.

    I like kimchi.

3. 버스 _____ 타야 해요.

    Beoseu _____ taya haeyo.

    I need to get on the bus.

4. 항상 당신 _____ 응원하겠습니다.

    Hangsang dangsin _____ eungwonhagetseumnida.

    I'll always cheer for you.

5. 저는 친구 _____ 도와줬어요.

    Jeoneun chingu _____ dowajwosseoyo.

    I helped my friend.

Practice Activity 6

Fill in the blanks with the correct word and appropriate marker:

Example:
나는 그 사람을 좋아한다.
Naneun geu sarameul joahanda.
I like that person.

1. 캐서린이 _____ 마셔요.
    (tea)

    Kaeseorini _____ masyeoyo.

    Katherine drinks tea.

2. 저는 _____ 타요.
    (taxi)

    Jeoneun _____ tayo.

    I ride the taxi.

3. 죄송한데 _____ 어디 있는지 아세요?
    (bus station)

    Joesonghande _____ eodi inneunji aseyo?

    Excuse me, do you know where the bus station is?

4. 혹시 _____ 어디에 있어요?
   (subway)

   Hoksi _____ eodie isseoyo?

   Excuse me, do you know where the subway is?

5. 저는 _____ 타야 돼요. 그런데 _____ 어디 있는지 모르겠어요.
   (train)   (station)

   Jeoneun _____ taya dwaeyo. Geureonde _____ eodi inneunji moreugesseoyo.

   I need to ride the train. But I don't know where the station is.

🎧 :DIALOGUE 3: **Where is the Market?**

Andrew asks a stranger how to get to Dongdaemun Market.

Andrew: Excuse me, do you know how to get to Dongdaemun Market?
          Jeogiyo! Hoksi dongdaemun sijang eotteoke ganeunji aseyo?
          저기요! 혹시 동대문 시장 어떻게 가는지 아세요?

Chulsu: Yes, you need to take line 5 from the station there.
          Ne, jeo yeogeseo ohoseon tamyeon dwaeyo.
          네, 저 역에서 5호선 타면 돼요.

Andrew: Thank you. What station do I need to get off at?
          Gamsahamnida! Hoksi eotteon yeogeseo naeryeoya doeneunji aseyo?
          감사합니다! 혹시 어떤 역에서 내려야 되는지 아세요?

Chulsu: Get off at Dongdaemun History and Culture Park.
          Dongdaemun yeoksamunhwagongwonyeogeseo naerimyeon dwaeyo.
          동대문 역사문화공원역에서 내리면 돼요.

Andrew: Thank you for helping me!
          Dowajusyeoseo gamsahamnida!
          도와주셔서 감사합니다!

Chulsu: No problem.
          Animnida!
          아닙니다!

🎧 New Vocabulary 3

market	시장 **sijang**
line	호선 **hoseon**
be done, become	되다/돼다 **doeda/dwaeda**

to get off	내리다 **naerida**
this (close to the speaker)	여기(이) **yeogi(i)**
that (close to the listener)	거기(그) **geogi(geu)**
that (not close to both the listener and speaker)	저기(저) **jeogi(jeo)**
perchance, maybe	혹시 **hoksi**
history	역사 **yeoksa**
culture	문화 **munhwa**
park	공원 **gongwon**

GRAMMAR NOTE Eliminating Markers

Sometimes there is enough information within a sentence that we can assume what the role of each word is without the need for markers. This is the case normally for short, simple sentences. For longer sentences it is best practice to use the appropriate markers to avoid confusion or misunderstanding. As you speak with Koreans, when and where to drop markers will become clearer and more natural, but let's look at a couple of situations where we could drop some markers.

Situations where we can eliminate markers

- When using personal pronouns as a subject.

  나는 영국사람이다. ➠ 나 영국사람이다.

  Naneun yeongguksaramida. ➠ **Na yeongguksaramida.**

  I am British. ➠ *I am British.*

- Locative markers can be dropped in casual conversations:

  공원에 가요. ➠ 공원 가요.

  Gongwone gayo. ➠ **Gongwon gayo.**

  I'm going to the park. ➠ *I'm going to the park.*

- If the meaning of the sentence is clear, we can drop both the subject and object markers in a sentence.

  나는 너를 좋아한다. ➠ 나 너 좋아한다.

  Naneun neoreul joahanda. ➠ **Na neo joahanda.**

  I like you. ➠ *I like you.*

Speakers of Korean often drop markers to make speaking as simple and concise as possible. If your subject and object are obvious, drop the markers. If the person you are talking to seems confused, restate your sentence with the markers added.

CULTURAL NOTE Bargaining and Korean Money

The Korean currency is the won (원 **won**) shown as ₩. The coins used are ₩10, ₩50, ₩100, ₩500, while the bills are ₩1,000, ₩5,000, ₩10,000 and ₩50,000. To give a really rough comparison ₩1,000 is usually equivalent to approximately $1 U.S.D., depending on the changing economies. Since we already learned numbers, let's review briefly and then add currency counters.

Say the following numbers out loud to review.

십	**sip**	10	만	**man**	10,000
백	**baek**	100	억	**eok**	100,000,000
천	**cheon**	1,000	조	**jo**	1,000,000,000,000

Korean uses combinations of 10,000 to express large numbers. So a million won would be expressed as 100 만원 **manwon** (백만원 **baengmanwon**) or a billion won would be 10 억원 **sip eogwon**. This can be really confusing to start with but as you practice you will start to get the hang of it.

There is a bargaining culture in Korean outdoor markets. While you will not be able to get any discounts at the supermarket or department stores, you may not want to settle for the first price the salesperson gives you at the market. Having an understanding of money and how it works will help, but remember that vendors at the market will be more willing to give you a better price if you have the cash in hand. You will have no chance to bargain if you only have a credit card. Another thing to remember is that they may give you a higher price because you are a foreigner. It might help to check out prices from a couple of different vendors to get a feel for the price of the item you're trying to buy. If you look like you know what you're talking about vendors will be more than willing to negotiate with you.

Practice Activity 7

Match the following Korean words with the appropriate English word.

1. 공원 **gongwon** _____   park

2. 거기 (그) **geogi (geu)** _____   history

3. 여기 (이) **yeogi (i)** _____   market

4. 역사 **yeoksa** _____   culture

5. 내리다 **naerida** _____   get off

6. 시장 sijang _____   there (close to listener)

7. 문화 munhwa _____   be done, become

8. 되다/돼다 doeda/dwaeda _____   here (close to speaker)

Practice Activity 8

Read the following sentences and eliminate markers to make it sound more natural.

1. 나는 영국사람이다. = _____.
   Naneun yeongguksaramida.
   I am British.

2. 민수는 여행하고 있어요. = _____.
   Minsuneun yeohaenghago isseoyo.
   Minsu is traveling.

3. 사라는 학교에 가고 있어요. = _____.
   Saraneun hakgyoe gago isseoyo.
   Sarah is going to school.

4. 철수는 한국으로 갔어요. = _____.
   Cheolsuneun hangukeuro gasseoyo.
   Chulsu went to South Korea.

Practice Activity 9

With a partner, practice saying the correct monetary amounts below:

Example:
    ₩1,500   = 천오백 원 **cheonobaek won**

1. ₩13,700   = _____

2. ₩48,000   = _____

3. ₩52,060   = _____

4. ₩890,700   = _____

5. ₩7 billion = _____

Hello!
Annyeonghaseyo?

Hello!
Annyeonghaseyo?

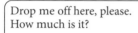

Please take me to Gangnam station.
Gangnamyeogeuro ga juseyo.

All right.
Ne, algetseumnida.

Drop me off here, please. How much is it?
Gisanim, yeogiseo naeryeo juseyo. Eolmayeyo?

It is 8,000 won.
Palcheonwonimnida.

The transaction is complete.
Gyesan da dwaetseumnida.

Thank you.
Gamsahamnida, gisanim.

Goodbye.
Ne, annyeonghi gaseyo.

LESSON 7
Using Public Transportation

🎧 ┊**DIALOGUE 1**┊ **Taxi Please!**

Peter travels to Gangnam station by taxi.

Peter: Hello!
Annyeonghaseyo?
안녕하세요?

Taxi driver: Hello!
Annyeonghaseyo?
안녕하세요?

Peter: Please take me to Gangnam station.
Gangnamyeogeuro ga juseyo.
강남역으로 가 주세요.

Taxi driver: All right.
Ne, algetseumnida.
네, 알겠습니다.

20 minutes later…

Peter: Drop me off here, please. How much is it?
Gisanim, yeogiseo naeryeo juseyo. Eolmayeyo?
기사님, 여기서 내려 주세요. 얼마예요?

Taxi driver: It is 8,000 won.
Palcheonwonimnida.
8천원입니다.

Peter: I will pay with cash.
Gyesaneun hyeongeumeuro halgeyo.
계산은 현금으로 할게요.

Taxi driver: The transaction is complete.
Gyesan da dwaetseumnida.
계산 다 됐습니다.

Peter: Thank you.
Gamsahamnida, gisanim.
감사합니다, 기사님.

Taxi driver: Goodbye!
Ne, annyeonghi gaseyo.
네, 안녕히 가세요.

New Vocabulary 1

driver	기사 **gisa**
honorific suffix	님 **nim**
empty car, vacant	빈차 **bincha**
credit card	(신용)카드 **(sinyong) kadeu**
cash	현금 **hyeongeum**
payment	계산 **gyesan**
right (direction)	오른 **oreun**
left (direction)	왼 **oen**
straight (direction)	직진 **jikjin**
direction	쪽 **jjok**

GRAMMAR NOTE **Indicating the Destination of a Ride**

When you are in Korea, you will want to visit many different places. Telling people where you want to go is important and simple by using these structures:

- Noun + (으)로 가 주세요 **(eu)ro ga juseyo** is used to politely tell someone where you want to go (Please take me to _____).

- Noun + 으로 가 주세요 **euro ga juseyo** is used when the noun ends in a consonant (e.g.: 서울역으로 가 주세요. **Seoulyeogeuro ga juseyo.** Please take me to Seoul Station).

- Noun + 로 가 주세요 **ro ga juseyo** is used when the noun ends in a vowel (e.g.: 연세대학교로 가 주세요. **Yeonsedaehakgyoro ga juseyo.** Please take me to Yonsei University).

The easiest way to tell someone, like a taxi driver, where to go is to use landmarks, subway stations, and directions:

홍대역으로 가 주세요.
Hongdaeyeogeuro ga juseyo.
Please take me to Hongdae Station.

경복궁으로 가 주세요.
Gyeongbokgungeuro ga juseyo.
Please take me to Gyeongbok Palace.

오른쪽으로 가 주세요.
Oreunjjogeuro ga juseyo.
Please go right.

Locating addresses in Korea can be quite confusing, even for Koreans! Use subway stations, landmarks, and directions to direct people to the general area you would like to travel to. When you arrive in the general destination, use directions, local businesses, restaurants and subway stations to specify exactly where you want to go.

What if you want to ask someone where he is going? Use the phrase "어디로 가요?" **Eodiro gayo?** (Where are you going?) to inquire as to where someone is going.

CULTURAL NOTE Calling and Tipping Taxi Drivers

Like many other countries, you can hail a taxi on the street. Korea has an abundance of taxis in major cities. Look for the sign "빈차" **bin cha**, which means "empty car." It will be displayed in red LED lights in the center of the windshield of vacant taxis. Nothing will be displayed if the taxi is full.

Be aware that in Korea there are several types of taxis: Standard Taxis (orange or silver), Deluxe Taxis (black), and International Taxis (orange with "international taxi" displayed on the side). Most taxi drivers do not speak English except for international taxi drivers.

Korea has a no tip culture. Don't worry, it is neither customary nor expected for taxi drivers to receive a tip. When you pay for a taxi fare, taxi drivers will give you back the exact change. You can usually pay by cash, credit card, or in Seoul with a t-money card for a taxi fare. Taxis are more expensive than the subway or bus; however, taxis are usually the fastest way to travel downtown (depending on the time of day) and the only way to travel late at night.

Practice Activity 1

Match the English words with the appropriate Korean translations.

1. straight (direction) _____   a. 빈차 **bin cha**

2. payment _____   b. 기사 **gisa**

3. cash _____   c. 계산 **gyesan**

4. direction _____   d. 직진 **jikjin**

5. empty car, vacant _____   e. 현금 **hyeongeum**

6. driver _____   f. 쪽 **jjok**

Practice Activity 2

Use the phrases below to practice telling a taxi driver where you want to go.

_____ (으)로 가 주세요. **(eu)ro ga juseyo.**

Please take me to (the) _____.

1. right direction
2. left direction
3. subway
4. Gyeongbok Palace
5. Hongdae Station

Practice Activity 3

Translate the sentences into Korean by using "_____ (으)로 가 주세요. "

1. Please take me to Seoul Station.   = _____.

2. Please take me to the airport.   = _____.

3. Please take me to the market.   = _____.

4. Please take me to Seoul University. = _____.

5. Please take me to Lotte World.   = _____.

🎧 DIALOGUE 2 **Getting on the Subway**

Peter learns how to take the subway.

Taeyang: Where are you going?
           Eodiro gaseyo?
           어디로 가세요?

James: I'm going to Yeouido! How do I get to Yeouido Station?
           Yeouidoro gayo! Yeouidoyeogeuro eotteoke gaya dwaeyo?
           여의도로 가요! 여의도역으로 어떻게 가야 돼요?

Taeyang: Take line 2 toward Hapjeong and get off at Yeongdeungpo-gu
           Office Station. From there, transfer to Line 5 towards Yeong-
           deungpo Market. If you go three stops you will arrive at Yeouido
           Station.
           **Hapjeong banghyangeuro ganeun ihoseoneul tago Yeongdeungpo-
           gucheongyeogeseo naeriseyo. Geogiseo yeongdeungposijang
           banghyangeuro ganeun ohoseoneuro hwanseunghaseyo. Se
           jeonggeojang gamyeon yeouidoyeogieyo.**

합정 방향으로 가는 이(2)호선을 타고, 영등포구청역에서 내리세요. 거기서 영등포시장 방향으로 가는 오(5)호선으로 환승하세요. 세 정거장 가면 여의 도역이에요.

James: At Yeouido Station what is my exit?
            Yeouidoyeogeseo myeot beon chulguro nagayo?
            여의도역에서 몇 번 출구로 나가요?

Taeyang: Get off at exit 2.
            Ibeon chulguro nagaseyo.
            이(2) 번 출구로 나가세요.

James: Thank you. Goodbye.
            Gamsahamnida. Annyeonghi gyeseyo.
            감사합니다. 안녕히 계세요.

Taeyang: Goodbye.
            Annyeonghi gaseyo.
            안녕히 가세요.

🎧 New Vocabulary 2

direction	방향 **banghyang**
subway station	역 **yeok**
subway stop	정거장 **jeonggeojang**
a number (gate no.1, gate no. 2, etc.)	-번 **beon**
counter (number of items)	-개 **gae**
subway	전철 **jeoncheol**
subway station exit/entrance	출구/입구 **chulgu/ipgu**
to transfer	환승하다 **hwanseunghada**

GRAMMAR NOTE Numbers and Counters

In Korean, specific counters are used for certain nouns. -개 **Gae**, -번 **beon**, and -명 **myeong** are some of the main counters used in Korean. -개 **Gae** is used generally as an "items" counter. -번 **Beon** is used as a counter for the number of times something was done. -명 **Myeong** is used as a counter for people.

Some other common counters are -권 **gwon** for the number of books, -마리 **mari** for the number of animals, -대 **dae** for the number of cars, and -장 **jang** for the number of papers.

Counters are mainly used with pure Korean Numbers (e.g., 하나 **hana** one, 둘 **dul** two, 셋 **set** three…); however, for larger numbers (more than the number 50), counters tend to use Sino-Korean numbers (e.g., 팔십 **palsip** eighty, 백 **baek** one hundred , 천 **cheon** one thousand). When using pure Korean numbers, you should be aware of some conjugation rules.

1. 둘 **dul** (two) drops the "ㄹ" **r** (e.g., 두 번 **du beon** "two times," 스물두 대 **seumuldu dae** "twenty-two machines").
2. 셋 **set** and 넷 **net** drop the "ㅅ" **s** at the bottom (e.g., 세 명 **se myeong** "three people," 네 개 **ne gae** "four things," 열네 장 **yeolle jang** "fourteen papers").

When you want to ask the number of things, you use 몇 **myeot** + counter 이에요/예요 **ieyo/yeyo** (e.g., 몇 개예요? **myeot gaeyeyo?** "How many things?," 몇 명이에요? **myeon myeongieyo?** "How many people?," 몇 마리예요? **myeon mariyeyo?** "How many animals?").

Here are some examples of common counters.

people	명 (한 명)	myeong (han myeong "one person")
animals	마리 (네 마리)	mari (ne mari "four animals")
books	권 (세 권)	gwon (se gwon "three books")
bottles	병 (여섯 병)	byeong (yeoseot byeong "six bottles")
glasses	잔 (다섯 잔)	jan (daseot jan "five glasses")
age	살 (여덟 살)	sal (yeodeol sal "eight years")

CULTURAL NOTE Personal Space

Personal space, in a country with limited land mass and 50+ million people, may not be equivalent to the amount of space you are comfortable with, especially in public areas and on public transportation. Generally, when a few people are on the bus, train, or subway, people will spread out to find an open seat; however, during rush hour, that is not the case. Subways and buses are crammed to the brim. Often, the space available is "standing room only."

Koreans expect to come in very close contact with other people every day, especially during rush hour. Because of this, people tend not to worry or apologize when personal space is invaded. Don't be offended if people bump into you and do not apologize. For Koreans, it is just a part of everyday life. There are unspoken rules in crowded spaces, however. On a very crowded subway or bus never look directly in the eyes of the person standing next to or near you and never try to strike up a conversation with them. To be squished together on a subway car is only acceptable if there is no attempt to get personal.

Practice Activity 4

Choose the appropriate counter from the box for the items listed.

명 myeong	개 gae	병 byeong	잔 jan	장 jang
권 gwon	번 beon	마리 mari	대 dae	채 chae

1. time _____

2. bottles _____

3. paper _____

4. cars _____

5. books _____

6. people _____

7. items _____

8. animals _____

9. buildings _____

10. glasses _____

Practice Activity 5

Read the following English sentences and match them with the correct Korean translation.

1. How many people? _____
   a. 몇 장이에요? **Myeot jangieyo?**

2. How many animals? _____
   b. 몇 권이에요? **Myeot gwonieyo?**

3. How many bottles? _____
   c. 몇 마리예요? **Myeon mariyeyo?**

4. How many pieces of paper? _____
   d. 몇 병이에요?
   Myeot byeongieyo?

5. How many times did you go? _____
   e. 몇 번 갔어요?
   Myeot beon gasseoyo?

6. How many books? _____
   f. 몇 명이에요?
   Myeon myeongieyo?

Practice Activity 6

Read the following questions and give the correct answer. An example is given.

A: 몇 권이에요? **Myeot gwonieyo?**
How many books?

B: 세 권이에요. (3) **Se gwonieyo**
Three books.

1. A: 몇 마리예요? **Myeon mariyeyo?**
   How many animals?

   B: _____ (5)

2. A: 몇 대예요? **Myeot daeyeyo?**
   How many cars?

   B: _____ (3)

3. A: 몇 명이에요? **Myeon myeongieyo?**
   How many people?

   B: _____ (12)

4. A: 몇 번 갔어요? **Myeot beon gasseoyo?**
   How many times did you go?

   B: _____ (8)

5. A: 몇 개예요? **Myeot gaeyeyo?**
   How many items?

   B: _____ (2)

6. A: 몇 장이에요? **Myeot jangieyo?**
   How many pieces of paper?

   B: _____ (1)

7. A: 몇 병이에요? **Myeot byeongieyo?**
   How many bottles?

   B: _____ (7)

🎧 **DIALOGUE 3** **The Express Train to Busan**

John plans to travel to Busan.

John: Hello!
Annyeonghaseyo?
안녕하세요?

Sales clerk: Hello! Where are you going?
Annyeonghaseyo? Eodiro gaseyo?
안녕하세요? 어디로 가세요?

John: Busan. What time does the train for Busan depart?
Busaniyo. Busanhaeng gichaneun myeot sie isseoyo?
부산이요. 부산행 기차는 몇 시에 있어요?

Sales clerk: The next train departs at 4 PM.
Daeum gichaneun ohu nesi imnida.
다음 기차는 오후 네(4)시 입니다.

John: When does it arrive at Busan?
Busane myeot sie dochakaeyo?
부산에 몇 시에 도착해요?

Sales clerk: It arrives at 6:36 PM.
Ohu yeoseot si samsibyuk(36) bune dochakamnida.
오후 여섯 (6)시 삼십육 (36)분에 도착합니다.

John: How much is a round-trip ticket?
Wangbogeun eolmayeyo?
왕복은 얼마예요?

Sales clerk: It's sixty thousand won.
Yungman won imnida.
육 (6)만 원 입니다.

John: Ok, I'll get two tickets for the train at 4 PM.
Geureom, nesi gicharo du jang juseyo.
그럼, 네(4)시 기차로 두(2) 장 주세요.

Sales clerk: All right, two tickets to Busan at 4 PM.
Ne, busanhaeng nesi gicharo du jang deurigetseumnida
네, 부산행 네 (4) 시 기차로 두 (2) 장 드리겠습니다.

John: Thank you.
Gamsahamnida
감사합니다.

New Vocabulary 3

train	기차 **gicha**
to arrive	도착하다 **dochakada**
train station	기차역 **gichayeok**
to purchase	구매하다 **gumaehada**
round trip	왕복 **wangbok**
one-way trip	편도 **pyeondo**
ticket	티켓 **tiket**
timetable	시간표 **siganpyo**
fare	요금 **yogeum**
train destination	-행 **haeng**

GRAMMAR NOTE **Locative Markers**

As you know, 에 **e** and 에서 **eseo** are the locative markers for Korean. 에 **E** and 에서 **eseo** have two different meanings. Let's review 에 **e** and how this particle is used so that you clearly understand the difference between 에 **e** and 에서 **eseo**. 에 **E** refers to the position, location, or existence of something. It can be translated as "in," "on," "at," or "to" depending on the context. In Lesson 5, you used it to indicate where an object exists. Below, you can see sentences using 에 **e** in a variety of ways.

학교에 가요.
Hakgyoe gayo.
*I am going **to** school.*

집에 가요.
Jibe gayo.
I am going home.

지하철에 있습니다.
Jihacheore itseumnida.
*She is **on** the subway.*

냉장고에 있어.
Naengjanggoe isseo.
*It is **in** the fridge.*

Do you remember from Lesson 6 that 에서 **eseo** means "in," "from," or "at"? It differs from 에 **e** since it is used when you refer to an action at a location.

미국에서 왔어요.
Migugeseo wasseoyo.
*I came **from** America.*

회사에서 일합니다.
Hoesaeseo ilhamnida.
*I work **in** a company.*

식당에서 김치를 먹어요.
Sikdangeseo gimchireul meogeoyo.
*I eat kimchi **at** a restaurant.*

Both locative markers are used differently, and most of the time, they cannot be used interchangeably.

CULTURAL NOTE What to See in Busan

Busan is a port city located on the southern tip of South Korea. It is known for its beaches, markets, and temples.

The world-famous Jagalchi Fish Market features fresh raw fish and seafood to use as ingredients and is also a place to grab a quick meal in one of the many market stalls. It is the largest and one of the oldest fish markets in Korea. As it is mostly run by women, the vendors are referred to as "Jalgalchi ajumma." To get to Jagalchi Market, take Busan subway line 1 to Jagalchi Station exit 10.

Haeundae Beach is the most famous beach in Korea and the most popular beach in Busan. The nearly two-kilometer long beach is wide with shallow waters, making it great for lounging on the beach or swimming in the ocean. People are attracted to Haeundae Beach all year round for local cultural events and festivals.

Beomeosa Temple, Gwangan Bridge, and Gamcheon Culture Village are all must-see places in Busan! The 1,300-year-old Beomeosa temple is one of the country's most well-known temples. The temple is located at the edge of the famous Geumjeong Mountain. Gwangan Bridge is the longest bi-level bridge over the ocean in Korea. The thousands of LED lights attached to the bridge showcase beautiful light shows. Lastly, Gamcheon Culture Village is a beautiful little place of colorful houses, painted murals, and creative art and shops.

Busan is a city full of deep culture, breathtaking sights, and relaxing getaways. There is much more to see and do in Busan, so go check it out!

Practice Activity 7

Fill in the blank with the correct meaning in English or Korean.

1. one-way trip   _____

2. timetable   _____

3. 왕복 **wangbok**   _____

4. train destination _____

5. 도착 **dochak**   _____

6. fare   _____

7. 구매 **gumae**   _____

Practice Activity 8

Circle the proper marker (에 **e** / 에서 **eseo**) for each statement.

1. I am going _____ Korea. 한국 （ 에 / 에서 ） 가요. **Hanguk _____ gayo.**

2. I am _____ school. 학교 （ 에 / 에서 ） 있어요. **Hakgyo _____ isseoyo.**

3. I eat kimchi _____ a restaurant.
   식당 (에 / 에서) 김치를 먹어요. **Sikdang _____ gimchireul meogeoyo.**

4. I work _____ Korea. 한국 （ 에 / 에서 ） 일합니다. **Hanguk _____ ilhamnida.**

5. She is _____ the subway.
   지하철 （ 에 / 에서 ） 있습니다. **Jihacheol _____ itseumnida.**

Practice Activity 9

Fill the blank with the correct marker.

1. 식당 _____ 파스타를 먹어요. **Sikdang _____ paseutareul meogeoyo.**
   I eat pasta _____ a restaurant.

2. 마크는 집 _____ 있어요. **Makeuneun jip _____ isseoyo.**
   Mark is _____ the house.

3. 한국 _____ 왔어요. **Hanguk _____ wasseoyo.** I am _____ Korea.

4. 회사 _____ 일합니다. **Hoesa _____ ilhamnida.** I work _____ a company.

5. 도서관 _____ 있어요. **Doseogwan _____ isseoyo.** I am _____ the library.

Practice Activity 10

Read the conversation without romanization and fill in the blank.

John: 안녕하세요?
         Hello?

판매원: a) _____ ? 어디로 가세요?
         Hello? Where are you going?

John: 부산이요. 부산   b) _____ 기차는 몇 시에 있어요?
         Busan. What time does the train for Busan depart?

판매원: 다음   c) _____ 는 오후 네 (4) 시 입니다.
         The next train departs at 4 PM.

John: 부산에 몇 시에   d) _____ 해요?
         When does it arrive at Busan?

판매원: 오후 여섯 (6) 시 삼십육 (36) 분에 도착합니다.
         It arrives at 6:36 PM.

John: e) _____ 은 얼마예요?
         How much is a round-trip ticket?

판매원: 육 (6) 만원 입니다.
         It's sixty thousand won.

John: 그럼, 네 (4) 시   f) _____ 로 두 (2) 장주세요.
         Ok, I'll get two tickets for the train at 4 PM.

판매원: 네,   g) _____ 행 네 (4) 시 기차로 두 (2) 장 드리겠습니다.
         All right, two tickets to Busan at 4 PM.

John: 감사합니다.
         Thank you.

LESSON 8
Talking About Pop Culture

🎧 DIALOGUE 1 **Discussing Music**

James and Eunkyung talk about Korean pop music.

James: Eunkyung, what type of music do you like—American music or Korean music?
Eungyeong ssi, miguk eumak joahaeyo, hanguk eumak joahaeyo?
은경 씨, 미국 음악 좋아해요, 한국 음악 좋아해요?

Eunkyung: I like Korean music!
Jeoneun hanguk eumageul joahaeyo!
저는 한국 음악을 좋아해요!

James: Oh really? Who is your favorite Korean singer?
Geuraeyo? Jeil joahaneun gasuneun nuguyeyo?
그래요? 제일 좋아하는 가수는 누구예요?

Eunkyung: My favorite Korean singer is IU.
Jega jeil joahaneun gasuneun IUyeyo.
제가 제일 좋아하는 가수는 IU예요.

James: Is she a K-pop singer or rapper?
K-Pop gasuyeyo, raepeoyeyo?
K-Pop 가수예요, 래퍼예요?

Eunkyung: She is a K-pop singer.
K-Pop gasuyeyo.
K-Pop 가수예요.

James: I will have to check her out!
Hanbeon deureobwaya doegenneyo!
한번 들어봐야 되겠네요!

Eunkyung: I have an extra ticket for the IU concert next weekend. Would you like to go with me?
Jega daeum jumal IU gongyeon yeobun tikesi isseoyo. Gachi gallaeyo?
제가 다음 주말 IU 공연 여분 티켓이 있어요. 같이 갈래요?

James: Wow, that sounds fun! Let's go!
Wa, jaemiitgenneyo! Gachi gayo!
와, 재미있겠네요! 같이 가요!

New Vocabulary 1

Korean pop music	**K-pop**
music	음악 **eumak**
the most	제일 **jeil**
favorite (to like)	좋아하다 **joahada**
singer	가수 **gasu**
rapper, rap artist	래퍼 **raepeo**
concert, performance	공연 **gongyeon**
extra	여분 **yeobun**

GRAMMAR NOTE Alternative Questions

An alternative question presents two or more possible answers to choose from while supposing that only one of the answers is true. An alternative question is used to ask someone to choose between the given choices. In English we ask alternative questions using the word "or."

Examples:
- Do you like American music or Korean music?
- Are you a freshman or a sophomore?
- Are you Australian or Taiwanese?
- Is your favorite Korean food, *bulgogi* or *tteokbokki*?

However, in Korean it is not necessary to use the word "or" to create alternative questions. Instead it is common to form an alternative question by presenting both options in two separate questions within the same sentence. Be sure to use rising intonation at the end of the first clause and falling intonation at the end of the second clause. The same questions that are asked above in English using "or" are asked in Korean below.

Examples:

미국 음악 좋아해요, 한국 음악 좋아해요?
Miguk eumak joahaeyo, hanguk eumak joahaeyo?
Do you like American music or Korean music?

일학년이에요, 이학년이에요?
Ilhangnyeonieyo, ihangnyeonieyo?
Are you a freshman or a sophomore? (Are you 1st grade or 2nd grade?)

호주 사람이에요, 대만 사람이에요?
Hoju saramieyo, daeman saramieyo?
Are you Australian or Taiwanese?

제일 좋아하는 한식이 불고기예요, 떡볶이예요?
Jeil joahaneun hansigi bulgogiyeyo, tteokbokkiyeyo?
What is your favorite Korean food, bulgogi *or* tteokbokki?

CULTURAL NOTE   한류 Hallyu the Korean Wave

It seems that anywhere you go you can find someone who is a fan of Korean music or Korean dramas. Korean pop music has spread across the globe over the last decade, permeating other countries and continents, spreading awareness and love for all things Korean. This phenomenon is called 한류 **hallyu**, or the Korean Wave. It literally means "flow of Korea," and it encompasses not just Korean music and television, but Korean film, language, fashion, cuisine, etc. For example, the Korean movie, *Parasite*, won the Oscar's Best Picture in 2020 and the Korean boy band BTS was named Artist of the Year at the 2021 American Music Awards. Korean skincare products are now being sold in

American stores such as Sephora, not to mention Korean barbecue restaurants popping up all over the world. This massive export of Korean culture and products has helped to significantly boost Korea's economy. It seems that with the steadily increasing popularity of Korean culture around the world the Korean wave is just getting started.

Practice Activity 1

Give the following meanings in Korean.

1. the most   _____

2. favorite (to like)   _____

3. rapper, rap artist   _____

4. singer   _____

5. concert, performance   _____

6. music   _____

Practice Activity 2

Create questions for the dialogue using the answers below. Then check out possible answer below.

1. Alan: _____?
   Akira: 저는 일본 사람이에요. **Jeoneun ilbon saramieyo.**

2. 지윤: _____?
   John: 저는 농구를 (basketball) 좋아해요. **Jeoneun nonggureul joahaeyo.**

3. Ben: _____?
   의견: 저는 강아지를 (puppy) 키워요. **Jeoneun gangajireul kiwoyo.**

4. 소현: _____?
   지수: 영화 보러 가요! **Yeonghwa boreo gayo!**

Possible Answers

1. Alan: Akira 씨, 일본 사람이에요, 중국 사람이에요?
   Akirassi, ilbon saramieyo, jungguk saramieyo?
   Akira, are you Japanese or Chinese?

2. 지윤: John 씨, 야구 좋아해요, 농구 좋아해요?
   Jon ssi, yagu joahaeyo, nonggu joahaeyo?
   John, do you like baseball or basketball?

3. Ben: 의견 씨, 강아지 키워요, 고양이 키워요?
   Uigeon ssi, gangaji kiwoyo, goyangi kiwoyo?
   Uigeon, do you keep a puppy or cat?

4. 소현: 지수 씨, 노래방에 갈까요, 영화 보러 갈까요?
   Jisu ssi, noraebange galkkayo, yeonghwa boreo galkkayo?
   Jisu, do you want to go to a karaoke or a movie?

Practice Activity 3

With a partner, translate the following alternative questions into Korean.

1. Do you want to take the bus or train?
2. Do you like pasta or pizza?
3. Do you like *bulgogi* (불고기) or *tteokbokki* (떡볶이)?
4. Are you a freshman or a sophomore?

🎧 **DIALOGUE 2 · Do You Like Korean dramas?**

Lewis and Jimin discuss which dramas to watch.

Jimin: Lewis, do you like Korean dramas?
Ruiseu ssi, hanguk deuramareul joahaeyo?
루이스 씨, 한국 드라마를 좋아해요?

Lewis: No, I don't watch Korean dramas.
Aniyo, hanguk deuramareul an bwayo.
아니요, 한국 드라마를 안 봐요.

Jimin: You should try watching one sometime. They are very helpful
when studying Korean.
**Geuraeyo? Hanbeon boseyo! Hangugeo gongbue doumi doel
geoyeyo.**
그래요? 한번 보세요! 한국어 공부에 도움이 될 거예요.

Lewis: Okay. Which one should I watch?
Joayo. Museun deuramareul bolkkayo?
좋아요. 무슨 드라마를 볼까요?

Jimin: I like *Romance is A Bonus Book*. It is a romantic comedy, and the
actors are very good.
**Jeoneun romaenseuneun byeolchaekburokeul joahageodeunyo.
Geu deuramaneun romaentik komidiyeyo. Naoneun baeudeuri
yeongireul jinjja jal haeyo.**
저는 "로맨스는 별책부록"을 좋아하거든요. 그 드라마는 로맨틱 코미디예요. 나
오는 배우들이 연기를 진짜 잘 해요.

Lewis: I don't like romantic comedies.
A, jeoneun romaentik komidireul byeollo an joahaeyo.
아, 저는 로맨틱 코미디를 별로 안 좋아해요.

Jimin: Then try watching *Jewel in the Palace*. It is a historical drama. It's a
little old, but it is famous around the world.
**Geureomyeon daejanggeumeul hanbeon boseyo. Sageugieyo.
jogeum oraedoen deuramainde segyejeogeuro yumyeonghaeyo.**
그러면 대장금을 한번 보세요. 사극이에요. 조금 오래된 드라마인데 세계적으로
유명해요.

Lewis: Wow, that sounds good. Where can I watch it?
Wa, joayo. Eodieseo bol su isseoyo?
와, 좋아요. 어디에서 볼 수 있어요?

Jimin: You can watch it on TV or use a streaming service. Do you want to watch with me tomorrow?
Tellebijeonina seuteuriming seobiseueseo bol su isseoyo. Naeil gachi bollaeyo?
텔레비전이나 스트리밍 서비스에서 볼 수 있어요. 내일 같이 볼래요?

Lewis: Tomorrow I have class, so I don't think I can. How about the weekend?
Naeil sueobi isseoseo gachi mot bol geot gatayo. Jumareun eottaeyo?
내일 수업이 있어서 같이 못 볼 것 같아요. 주말은 어때요?

Jimin: Yeah, that works. Let's do it on the weekend!
Ne, joayo. Jumare gachi bwayo!
네, 좋아요. 주말에 같이 봐요!

New Vocabulary 2

drama	드라마	**deurama**
actor	배우	**baeu**
act/performance	연기	**yeongi**
to see/watch	보다	**boda**
historical drama	사극	**sageuk**
famous	유명하다	**yumyeonghada**
old	오래되다	**oraedoeda**
worldwide/global	세계적	**segyejeok**
television	텔레비전	**tellebijeon**
streaming service	스트리밍서비스	**seuteuriming seobiseu**

GRAMMAR NOTE   Negative Adverbs

As you learned briefly in Lesson 3, there are many ways to form a negative sentence, in Korean. Let's review. One common way to make a sentence negative is by using the ending -지 않다 **ji anta** with a verb or an adjective. One can also show the inability to do something by using the phrase -ㄹ 수 없다 **r su eopda.**

Examples:
저는 김치를 먹지 않아요.
Jeoneun gimchireul meokji anayo.
I do not eat kimchi.

저는 김치를 먹을 수 없어요.
Jeoneun gimchireul meogeul su eopseoyo.
I cannot eat kimchi.

In addition to the examples above, the words 안 **an** and 못 **mot** can be placed before the final verb or adjective in order to make the sentence negative. In this case, 안 **an** and 못 **mot** act as negative adverbs in the sentence. 안 **An** is equivalent to the phrase "do not" in English, and 못 **mot** is equivalent to the phrase "cannot."

Examples:

저는 김치를 안 먹어요.
Jeoneun gimchireul an meogeoyo.
I do not eat kimchi.

저는 김치를 못 먹어요.
Jeoneun gimchireul mon meogeoyo.
I cannot eat kimchi.

The meaning of sentences containing -지 않다 **ji anta** and 안 **an** is essentially the same. In both cases the decision is a choice. The same is true for 못 **mot** and -ㄹ 수 없다 **r su eopda**. In both cases the decision seems to be out of the speakers' control. But there are instances where it will be more natural to use either 안 **an** /못 **mot** or -지 않다 **ji anta** / -ㄹ 수 없다 **r su eopda**. At this point you can use them interchangeably, and over time in your study of Korean, you will develop a feel for when it is appropriate to use one or the other.

CULTURAL NOTE **Who's Watching?**

When we hear about the Korean Wave, the first thing that usually comes to mind is the music. K-Pop has been successful all over the world and continues to grow, but what many do not realize is that Korean dramas achieved success outside of the Korean peninsula before the widespread popularity of K-Pop.

In the early 2000s viewers all over Asia started turning to Korean TV dramas for entertainment. One of the most notable dramas of this time was *Winter Sonata*, which was produced by the Korean channel KBS2. *Winter Sonata* was able to gain a large following in countries such as China, Japan, and others in Southeast Asia and eventually gained popularity in Russia and parts of the Middle East. Korean dramas also quickly gained popularity in Latin America, likely due to the fact that the content and emotion in the Korean shows is similar to that of the soap operas that are popular in those countries. Korean dramas are becoming very popular in the United States and Europe and are becoming more easily accessible through streaming services such as Netflix. Korean dramas have a little bit of everything. There is romance, comedy, drama, and action which provides enjoyable shows for all kinds of people.

Practice Activity 4

Match the English words with their appropriate Korean translations.

1. old _____   a. 배우 **baeu**

2. famous _____   b. 연기 **yeongi**

3. act/performance _____   c. 사극 **sageuk**

4. worldwide/global _____   d. 유명하다 **yumyeonghada**

5. historical drama _____   e. 오래되다 **oraedoeda**

6. actor _____   f. 세계적 **segyejeok**

Practice Activity 5

Circle the appropriate adverb (안 **an** / 못 **mot**) for each statement.

1. I do not eat kimchi.
   저는 김치를 (안 / 못) 먹어요. **Jeoneun gimchireul _____ meogeoyo.**

2. I do not watch Korean dramas.
   저는 한국 드라마를 (안 / 못) 봐요. **Jeoneun hanguk dramareul _____ bwayo.**

3. Seungwoo cannot take this class.
   승우는 이 수업을 (안 / 못) 들어요. **Seunguneun i sueobeul _____ deureoyo.**

4. Minyoung does not eat Japanese food.
   민영 씨는 일본 음식을 (안 / 못) 먹어요.
   Minyeong ssineun ilbon eumsik _____ meogeoyo.

Practice Activity 6

Create negative responses to the following questions using the negative adverb 안 **an.**

1. A: 일본 음식 많이 먹어요? **Ilbon eumsik mani meogeoyo?**
      Do you eat Japanese food often?

   B: _____

2. A: 그 여배우는 (actress) 예뻐요? **Geu yeobaeuneun yeppeoyo?**
      Is the actress beautiful?

   B: _____

3.   A: K-Pop 많이 들어요? **K-Pop mani deureoyo?**
     Do you listen to K-Pop often?

     B: _____

> **Possible Responses**
> 1.   아니요, 일본 음식을 안 먹어요.
>   **Aniyo, ilbon eumsigeul an meogeoyo.**
>   No, I don't eat Japanese food.
>
> 2.   아니요, 그 여배우는 안 예뻐요.
>   **Aniyo, geu yeobaeuneun an yeppeoyo.**
>   No, the actress is not pretty.
>
> 3.   아니요, 케이팝 (K-Pop)을 안 들어요.
>   **Aniyo, keipabeul an deureoyo.**
>   No, I don't listen to K-Pop.

Practice Activity 7

Create negative responses to the following questions using the negative adverb 못 **mot**.

1.   A: 주말에 서울에 놀러 갈까요? **Jumare seoure nolleo galkkayo?**
     Do you want to go to Seoul this weekend?

     B: _____

2.   A: 오늘 수업에 가요? **Oneul sueobe gayo?**
     Are you going to class today?

     B: _____

3.   A: 매운 음식 잘 먹어요? **Maeun eumsik jal meogeoyo?**
     Do you like spicy food?

     B: _____

4.   A: 어제 숙제를 다 했어요? **Eoje sukjereul da haesseoyo?**
     Did you do all your homework yesterday?

     B: _____

🎧 DIALOGUE 3 Let's Go to Lotte World!

Jenny and Yuna plan to go to Lotte World on a day they don't have class.

Yuna: Jenny, do you have plans tomorrow?
Jeni ssi, naeil mwo haeyo?
Jenny 씨, 내일 뭐 해요?

Jenny: I don't have class, so I'm just going to rest. What are you doing?
Sueobi eopseoseo geunyang swil geot gatayo. Yuna ssineunyo?
수업이 없어서 그냥 쉴 것 같아요. 윤아 씨는요?

Yuna: I'm going to Lotte World with Jack and Junho.
Jeoneun jaekgwa junhorang rotde woldeue gal geoyeyo.
저는 Jack과 준호랑 롯데 월드에 갈 거예요.

Jenny: That sounds fun. But who is Junho?
Jaemiitgetda! Geunde junhoneun nuguyeyo?
재미있겠다! 근데 준호는 누구예요?

Yuna: Junho is Jack's roommate.
Jaegui rummeiteuyeyo.
Jack의 룸메이트예요.

Jenny: Oh, I see. I have never been to Lotte World. What do you do there?
Geuraeyo. Jeoneun rotde woldeue ga bon jeogi eopseoyo. Mwo haneun gosieyo?
그래요. 저는 롯데 월드에 가 본 적이 없어요. 뭐 하는 곳이에요?

Yuna: It is an amusement park. There are roller coasters, rides, good food, and an arcade.
Rotde woldeuneun nori gongwonieyo. Rolleokoseuteowa dareun nori gigureul tal su itgo, masinneun meogeulgeorido manayo. Geurigo akeideu geimjangdo isseoyo.
롯데 월드는 놀이 공원이에요. 롤러코스터와 다른 놀이 기구를 탈 수 있고, 맛있는 먹을거리도 많아요. 그리고 아케이드 게임장도 있어요.

Jenny: Is admission expensive?
Ipjangnyoneun bissayo?
입장료는 비싸요?

Yuna: It's not too expensive.
Byeollo bissaji anayo.
별로 비싸지 않아요.

Jenny: Alright. Let's go!
Joayo. Gachi gayo!
좋아요. 같이 가요!

New Vocabulary 3

to rest	쉬다 **swida**
Lotte World	롯데 월드 **rotde woldeu**
roommate	룸메이트 **rummeiteu**
amusement park	놀이 공원 **nori gongwon**
roller coaster	롤러코스터 **rolleokoseuteo**
ride (amusement park)	놀이 기구 **nori gigu**
food	먹을거리 **meogeulgeori**
arcade	아케이드 **akeideu**
admission fee	입장료 **ipjangnyo**
expensive	비싸다 **bissada**

GRAMMAR NOTE Expressing Possession (Part One)

The possessive pronouns such as "mine, yours, his, hers, theirs," etc. do not exist in Korean.

The particle 의 **ui** is used to show possession. It literally means "of" but is used in the same situations as the possessive 's in English.

Examples:

Jack의 룸메이트
Jaegui rummeiteu
Jack's roommate (Lit., the roommate of Jack)

지수의 친구
Jisuui chingu
Jisu's friend

책의 내용
chaegui naeyong
The book's contents/the contents of the book

나라의 대통령
naraui daetongnyeong
The country's president/the president of the country

Because possessive pronouns are not used, if you want to show possession of an object without actually naming the object itself, you use the word 것 **geot** which literally means "thing" or "stuff." For example, if you want to say "that's Minji's" you would combine her name with 것 **geot** to create the phrase "민지(의) 것" **Minji(ui) geot** (Minji's thing). In this case the participle 의 **ui** is often omitted.

Examples:

그 가방은 민지 것이에요.

Geu gabangeun minji geosieyo.

That bag is Minji's.

이 핸드폰은 민지 것이에요.

I haendeuponeun minji geosieyo.

The phone is Minji's.

Phrases that contain "것" **geot** can sound less formal and more colloquial by changing "것" **geot** to "거" **geo**. 거 **Geo** is more common in casual conversations. As you practice speaking with native Korean speakers, you will get a feel for when it is appropriate to use one or the other.

Examples:

그 책은 민지 거예요.

Geu chaegeun Minji geoyeyo.

The book is Minji's.

그 가방은 민지 거예요.

Geu gabangeun Minji geoyeyo.

That bag is Minji's.

이 핸드폰은 민지 거예요.

I haendeuponeun Minji geoyeyo.

The phone is Minji's.

CULTURAL NOTE Lotte World

Lotte World is an amusement park in Sincheon-dong, Seoul. Opened in 1989, the park gets around 7.3 million visitors per year. It is the world's largest indoor theme park. It also includes an outdoor amusement park called Magic Island, an artificial island. There are all kinds of rides and attractions as well as a lake connected by monorail. There are also shopping malls, a multitude of restaurants, a hotel, a museum, and a few movie theaters. The current ticket price for an adult is 57,000 won for a Universal pass which gives you access to Lotte World and the folk museum. That price, which is close to $50 USD, allows visitors to enjoy a day of entertainment for significantly less money than theme parks in the United States such as Disneyland and Universal Studios. Lotte World is also located next to Lotte Tower which is the tallest building in Korea (sixth tallest in the world) measuring 1,821 feet high. Lotte Tower is another popular tourist attraction as it offers tours to the top level to look at a 360-degree view of Seoul from almost 2,000 feet above the city. Lotte World is a fun destination for anyone visiting Seoul who wants a great entertainment experience. It is easily accessible by subway on Line 2 Jamsil Station gate 4 or Line 8 Jamsil Station gate 4.

Practice Activity 8

Match the English words with their appropriate Korean translations.

1. 롯데 월드 **rotde woldeu** _____   a. food

2. 입장료 **ipjangnyo** _____   b. to rest

3. 비싸다 **bissada** _____   c. Lotte World

4. 놀이 공원 **nori gongwon** _____   d. ride (at an amusement park)

5. 놀이 기구 **nori gigu** _____   e. amusement park

6. 먹을거리 **meogeulgeori** _____   f. expensive

7. 쉬다 **swida** _____   g. admission

Practice Activity 9

Translate the following phrases into Korean using the particle 의 **ui**.

1. culture of Korea   _____

2. Jake's major   _____

3. younger brother's shoes _____

4. Minji's siblings   _____

5. friend of Jisu   _____

Practice Activity 9

Translate the following sentences into Korean.

1. Suzy is my roommate.   _____

2. That credit card is Jack's.   _____

3. Jake is my younger brother.   _____

4. The computer is Minji's.   _____

5. That television is Minyeong's. _____

Jihun, I'm really hungry! Shall we go get something to eat?

Jihun ssi, jeoneun jinjja baegopayo! Bap meogeureo galkkayo?

Sure, sounds good! I'm also hungry. What shall we eat?

Ne, joayo! Jeodo baegopayo. Mwol meogeulkkayo?

I want to eat pork belly. Is there a meat restaurant (house) around here?

Jeoneun samgyeopsareul meokgo sipeoyo. I geuncheoe gogitjibi innayo?

Yes. There is a good one near the department store. Let's go there.

Ne. Baekwajeom geuncheoe joeun dega isseoyo. Geogiro gapsida.

OK. Shall we go by subway? Or shall we go by bus?

Joayo. Jihacheollo galkkayo? Beoseuro galkkayo?

Let's go by subway. It will be faster.

Jihacheollo gapsida. Geuge deo ppallayo.

LESSON 9
Dining Out

🎧 `DIALOGUE 1` **Where Shall We Eat?**

John and Jihun discuss what to eat for lunch.

John: Jihun, I'm really hungry! Shall we go get something to eat?
Jihun ssi, jeoneun jinjja baegopayo! Bap meogeureo galkkayo?
지훈 씨, 저는 진짜 배고파요! 밥 먹으러 갈까요?

Jihun: Sure, sounds good! I'm also hungry. What shall we eat?
Ne, joayo! Jeodo baegopayo. Mwol meogeulkkayo?
네, 좋아요! 저도 배고파요. 뭘 먹을까요?

John: I want to eat pork belly. Is there a meat restaurant (house) around here?
Jeoneun samgyeopsareul meokgo sipeoyo. I geuncheoe gogitjibi innayo?
저는 삼겹살을 먹고 싶어요. 이 근처에 고기집이 있나요?

Jihun: Yes. There is a good one near the department store. Let's go there.
Ne. Baekwajeom geuncheoe joeun dega isseoyo. Geogiro gapsida.
네. 백화점 근처에 좋은 데가 있어요. 거기로 갑시다.

John: OK. Shall we go by subway? Or shall we go by bus?
Joayo. Jihacheollo galkkayo? Beoseuro galkkayo?
좋아요. 지하철로 갈까요? 버스로 갈까요?

Jihun: Let's go by subway. It will be faster.
Jihacheollo gapsida. Geuge deo ppallayo.
지하철로 갑시다. 그게 더 빨라요.

🎧 **New Vocabulary 1**

to be hungry	배고프다 baegopeuda
rice, food	밥 bap
pork belly	삼겹살 samgyeopsal
vicinity	근처 geuncheo
restaurant specializing in meat	고기집 gogitjib
department store	백화점 baekwajeom
place	데 de

GRAMMAR NOTE   **By Means Of**

The particle (으)로 (**eu**)**ro** (by means of) marks the method or tool by which an action is completed. This particle is often used to indicate means of transportation, just as in the previous dialogue and in the following examples:

자동차로 가다 **jadongcharo gada**   to go by means of car
택시로 가다 **taeksiro gada**   to go by means of taxi
비행기로 오다 **bihaenggiro oda**   to come by means of plane

The (으)로 (**eu**)**ro** particle also carries the meaning of "by means of" when it is used to mark the instrument or tool used to complete an action, such as in the following examples:

볼펜으로 쓰다 **bolpeneuro sseuda**   to write by means of a ball point pen
한국어로 말하다 **hangugeoro malhada**   to speak in (by means of) Korean
오븐으로 요리하다 **obeuneuro yorihada** to cook by means of an oven

Remembering that the particle (으)로 (**eu**)**ro** has additional meanings other than "by means of" can help avoid confusion. For example, in the previous dialogue, 지훈 **Jihun** used this particle to mark the place (the meat restaurant over there by the department store) to which they would go.

"으" **Eu** is added when the last syllable of a preceding word ends with a consonant (e.g., 볼펜으로 **bolpeneuro**, 오븐으로 **obeuneuro**). However, "ㄹ" **r** acts differently. Even though "ㄹ" is a consonant, "로" **ro** comes after "ㄹ" **r** (e.g., 연필로 **yeonpillo** "with a pencil").

CULTURAL NOTE   **Foreigner Favorites**

Although in general Korean cuisine is spicier and saltier than typical Western cuisine, most foreigners who expose themselves to traditional foods find themselves enjoying many dishes, some of which are pleasantly mild and sweet. Although a complete list of these "foreigner favorites" is beyond the scope of this book, here are some of the most popular:

- 불고기 **Bulgogi:** Marinated in a sweet and savory sauce, this Korean barbequed beef dish is loved by Koreans and foreigners alike. Many tour groups in Korea will order this dish because of its widespread appeal. It is easy to find this meal in both restaurants and Korean homes alike.
- 비빔밥 **Bibimbab:** The words of this dish literally mean "stirred rice," and that is exactly what is done when eating this dish. Just stir a colorful and delicious variety of fresh vegetables, meat or egg, a dash of sesame oil, and just a little bit of Korean hot pepper paste (고추장 **gochujang**) into

a hot bowl of rice. This dish is served in many places with various fresh ingredients, yet it always has its distinctive, delicious taste. This is a great dish with a medium level of spiciness, for those who are nervous about the spiciness of other Korean dishes. Chances are that once you take your first bite, you won't be able to put your spoon down.

- 김밥 **Gimbab**: The appearance and taste of this rolled up dish will remind you of sushi, but there is no raw fish. Instead, thin strips of a delectable meat are placed with ingredients such as carrot, cucumber, pickled radish and imitation crab meat on a square of rice-covered seaweed. The squares are then rolled up and cut into bite-sized pieces like sushi—a perfect size for grabbing them with chopsticks. One roll makes a good snack, or two rolls with side dishes make a delicious meal.

- 삼겹살 **Samgyeopsal**: This dish is a lot like bacon, as it is made from pork belly, but it is sliced more thickly and isn't as smoky or salty. In fact, part of the thrill of this dish is that most restaurants let you cook it yourself—right at the table where you are sitting. Countless buffets specializing in serving this meat with lettuce and sauces line the streets of Korean city centers. This is definitely something to experience on your next trip to Korea.

Practice Activity 1

Fill in the blanks with the particle 로 **ro** or (으)로 (**eu**)**ro** ("by means of," to indicate means of transportation).

1. 기차 _____ 갑시다. **Gicha _____ gapsida.**
   Let's go by train.

2. 백화점에 택시 _____ 왔어요. **Baekwajeome taeksi _____ wasseoyo.**
   I came to the department store by taxi.

3. 제주도에 비행기 _____ 갈까요? **Jejudoe bihaengki _____ galkkayo?**
   Shall we go to Jeju island by plane?

4. 버스 _____ 가면 편해요. **Beoseu _____ gamyeon pyeonhaeyo.**
   It is convenient to take a bus.

5. 일본에 배 _____ 갔어요. **Ilbone bae _____ gasseoyo.**
   I went to Japan by ship.

Practice Activity 2

Fill in the blanks with the particle 로 **ro** or (으)로 (**eu**)**ro** ("by means of," to mark the equipment used to complete an action).

1. 연필 _____ 필기를 하세요. **Yeonpil _____ pilgireul haseyo.**
   Take notes with a pencil.

2. 오븐 _____ 닭고기를 구웠어요. **Obeun _____ dakgogireul guwosseoyo.**
   I baked chicken using an oven.

3. 스마트폰 _____ 게임을 했어요. **Seumateupon _____ geimeul haesseoyo.**
   I played the game on my smartphone.

4. 노트북 _____ 영화를 봤어요. **Noteubuk _____ yeonghwareul bwasseoyo**
   I saw a movie on my laptop.

5. 손 _____ 사과를 잡았어요. **Son _____ sagwareul jabasseoyo.**
   I grabbed an apple with my hand.

Practice Activity 3 **Grammar review**

Read the sentences below and identify if (으)로 (**eu**)**ro** is used to mark means of transportation, the equipment to complete an action, or the place.

1. 제 집으로 오세요. **Je jibeuro oseyo.**
   Come over to my house.

2. 신용카드로 고기를 샀어요. **Sinyongkadeuro gogireul sasseoyo.**
   I bought meat using a credit card.

3. 자전거로 가면 빨라요. **Jajeongeoro gamyeon ppallayo.**
   It's faster to go by bike.

4. 저는 호텔로 갈게요. **Jeoneun hotello galgeyo.**
   I will go to the hotel.

5. 젓가락 (chopsticks) 으로 밥을 먹었어요.
   Jeotgarak (chopsticks) **euro babeul meogeosseoyo.**
   I had a meal with chopsticks.

🎧 DIALOGUE 2 **How to Order Food**

Sara does not know how to order Korean food and seeks help from a waiter.

Waiter: Welcome to Koryo Restaurant. How many?
  Eoseooseyo. Goryeosikdangimnida. Myeot buniseyo?
  어서오세요. 고려식당입니다. 몇 분이세요?

Sara: One.
  Han myeongiyo.
  한 명이요.

Waiter: Please have a seat here. What would you like to order?
  Ne. Ijjogeuro anjeuseyo. Jumunhasigesseoyo?
  네. 이쪽으로 앉으세요. 주문하시겠어요?

Sara: I'm not familiar with Korean food. Do you have any recommendations?
  Jega hansige daehe jal mollayo. Mwoga masisseoyo?
  제가 한식에 대해 잘 몰라요. 뭐가 맛있어요?

Waiter: Do you like spicy food?
  Maeun geo jal deuseyo?
  매운 거 잘 드세요?

Sara: No. Yesterday I tried *kimchijjigae*, but it was too spicy.
            Aniyo. Eoje gimchijjigaereul meogeonneunde neomu maewosseoyo.
            아니요. 어제 김치찌개를 먹었는데 너무 매웠어요.

Waiter: I see. If so, I recommend *bulgogi* or *doenjangjjigae*.
            Geureoseyo? Geureomyeon bulgogina doenjangjjigaereul deuseyo.
            그러세요? 그러면 불고기나 된장찌개를 드세요.

Sara: *Bulgogi*? I've heard a lot about *bulgogi*. How much is it?
            A, bulgogie daehae mani deureobwasseoyo. Eolmayeyo?
            아, 불고기에 대해 많이 들어봤어요. 얼마예요?

Waiter: For one person it is 6,000 won.
            Ilinbune yukcheon(6000)wonieyo.
            1인분에 6000원이에요.

Sara: O.K. then, I'll take a serving of *bulgogi*!
            Geureomyeon bulgogi hana juseyo!
            그러면 불고기 하나 주세요!

🎧 New Vocabulary 2

welcome	어서오세요	**eoseooseyo**
honorific counting word for people	분	**bun**
general counting word for people	명	**myeong**
Korean food	한식	**hansik**
about, to regard	대하다	**daehada**
to be spicy	맵다	**maepda**
honorable form of 먹다 (to eat)	드시다	**deusida**
kimchijjigae, a spicy stew made of kimchi, onion, tofu, meat and kimchi juice	김치찌개	**gimchijjigae**
doenjangjjiage – bean paste stew	된장찌개	**doenjangjjigae**
how much (adverb)	얼마	**eolma**
counter for number of servings (e.g., 4 인분 means a dish prepared for 4 people)	인분	**inbun**

GRAMMAR NOTE   Irregular Verbs

Most Korean verbs are conjugated following typical rules (see Lesson 4), but there are several categories of verbs that conjugate in irregular ways under certain circumstances. For example, in the dialogue above, the underlined irregular verb, 듣다 **deutda**, follows the rule described below. Here are descriptions of the seven types of irregular verbs:

ㄷ **D** irregular verbs: Some, but not all verbs ending in ㄷ **d** conjugate irregularly in some circumstances. There is no rule for which verbs conjugate regularly and which conjugate irregularly; the exceptions must be memorized.

Common verbs that conjugate normally and not irregularly include 받다 **bat-da** (to receive), 닫다 **datda** (to close), 믿다 **mitda** (to believe), and 얻다 **eotda** (to obtain).

In the irregular conjugation, the ㄷ **d** with which the verb stem ends changes to a ㄹ **r** when the conjugation starts with a vowel. For example, the verb 듣다 **deutda** (to listen) changes to 들었어요 **deureosseoyo** (I listened) because the conjugation (었어요 **eosseoyo**) begins with a vowel. However, it does not change and remains a ㄷ **d** when the conjugation starts with a consonant. For example, the verb 듣다 **deutda** conjugates normally as 듣겠어요 **deutgesseoyo** (I will listen) as the conjugation (겠어요 **gesseoyo**) begins with a consonant. More examples follow:

Korean (basic form)/ English	Present simple	Past	Future (will)	Past (adj.)	Future (adj.)
걷다 **geotda** (to walk)	걸어요 **georeoyo**	걸었어요 **georeosseoyo**	걷겠어요 **geotgesseoyo**	걸은 **georeun**	걸을 **georeul**
싣다 **sitda** (to load)	실어요 **sireoyo**	실었어요 **sireosseoyo**	싣겠어요 **sitgesseoyo**	실은 **sireun**	실을 **sireul**
묻다 **mutda** (to ask)	물어요 **mureoyo**	물었어요 **mureosseoyo**	묻겠어요 **mutgesseoyo**	물은 **mureun**	물을 **mureul**

* **Note:** 요 **yo** is a general honorific word ending and used here to show examples when -어 / 아 **eo/a** comes in conjugation.

ㄹ **r irregular verbs:** All words that end with a ㄹ **r** drop the ㄹ **r** when followed by a ㄴ **n**, ㅂ **b**, or ㅅ **s**. An example of this rule can be seen in the vocabulary word 드시다 **deusida** from this lesson. Originally, this word stems from the word 들다 **deulda**, meaning "to raise." However, when using (으)시다 (**eu**)**sida** for honorification, the (ㄹ) **r** is dropped because the conjugation begins with a ㅅ **s** to become 드시다 **deusida**. More examples can be found below:

Korean (basic form)/ English	Present continuous	Past (with honorific particle 시 si)	Future (will)	Past (adj.)	Future (adj.)
살다 **salda** (to live)	사는 **saneun**	사셨어요 **sasyeosseoyo**	살겠어요 **salgesseoyo**	산 **san**	살 **sal**
팔다 **palda** (to sell)	파는 **paneun**	파셨어요 **pasyeosseoyo**	팔겠어요 **palgesseoyo**	판 **pan**	팔 **pal**
울다 **ulda** (to cry)	우는 **uneun**	우셨어요 **usyeosseoyo**	울겠어요 **ulgesseoyo**	운 **un**	울 **ul**

ㅂ *b* **irregular verbs:** Most verbs ending with a ㅂ **b** conjugate differently when followed by a vowel. In these cases, the ㅂ **b** is transformed into the vowel 우 **u**. Not all verbs behave the same, however, those that do not follow this rule must be memorized. Common verbs that conjugate normally and do not drop the ㅂ **b** include 입다 **ipda** (to wear), 잡다 **japda** (to catch), 좁다 **jopda** (to be narrow) and 넓다 **neolda** (to be wide).

In the dialogue for this section, Sara correctly followed the irregular conjugation rules for 맵다 **maepda**. In this case, where the conjugation begins with a vowel, the ㅂ **b** becomes 우 **u** (맵 **maeb** ⇒ 매우 **maeu**), then the tense marker 었 **eot** and the word ending 어요 **eoyo** is applied for the final result of 매웠어요 **maewosseoyo**. Below are more examples of how to conjugate ㅂ irregular verbs:

Korean (basic form)/ English	Present simple	Past	Future (will)	Past (adj.)	Future (adj.)
눕다 **nupda** (to lie down)	누워요 **nuwoyo**	누웠어요 **nuwosseoyo**	눕겠어요 **nupgesseoyo**	누운 **nuun**	누울 **nuul**
덥다 **deopda** (to be hot)	더워요 **deowoyo**	더웠어요 **deowosseoyo**	덥겠어요 **deopgesseoyo**	더운 **deoun**	더울 **deoul**
밉다 **mipda** (to hate)	미워요 **miwoyo**	미웠어요 **miwosseoyo**	밉겠어요 **mipgesseoyo**	미운 **miun**	미울 **miul**

* **Note:** The verbs 돕다 **dopda** (to help) and 곱다 **gopda** (to be beautiful) are conjugated by replacing the ㅂ **b** with 오 **o** instead of 우 **u** in conjugations

requiring the addition of 아 **a** or 어 **eo** (e.g., 도왔어요 **dowasseoyo**, 고와서 **gowaseo**). In other conjugations such as (ㄴ **n** / 은 **eun**), (으면 **eumyeon**), etc., they conjugate according to the normal irregular pattern (e.g., 고운 **goun**, 도 우면 **doumyeon**).

르 *reu* irregular verbs: Verbs ending with 르 **reu** change form when followed by conjugations with the 아 **a** / 어 **eo** pattern. In such cases, these verbs receive an extra ㄹ **r** on the syllable preceding the 르, **reu** and then are conjugated accordingly. For example, in the dialogue for this lesson when Sara mentions that she doesn't know what Korean food is good, she correctly conjugated the verb 모르다 **moreuda** by first adding the extra ㄹ **r** (모르 **moreu** ⇒ 몰르 **molleu**), then following the conjugation rule of adding the word-ending (아 **a** / 어 **eo**) 요 **yo** to achieve the final result, 몰라요 **mollayo**. All verbs ending with "르" **reu** follow this rule, except for one word; ironically, the word that does not follow the irregular pattern is the word for "to follow," or "따르다" **ttareuda**. "따르다" **Ttareuda** is conjugated normally without adding an extra ㄹ **r**. Below are more examples of irregular conjugations:

Korean (basic form)/ English	Present simple	Past	Future (will)	Past (adj.)	Future (adj.)
빠르다 **ppareuda** (to be fast)	빨라요 **ppalayo**	빨랐어요 **ppallasseoyo**	빠르겠어요 **ppareugesseoyo**	빠른 **ppareun**	빠를 **ppareul**
부르다 **bureuda** (to call)	불러요 **bulleoyo**	불렀어요 **bulleosseoyo**	부르겠어요 **bureugesseoyo**	부른 **bureun**	부를 **bureul**
다르다 **dareuda** (to be different)	달라요 **dallayo**	달랐어요 **dallasseoyo**	다르겠어요 **dareugesseoyo**	다른 **dareun**	다를 **dareul**

ㅅ *s* irregular verbs: Many words that end with a ㅅ **s** have the ㅅ **s** dropped when followed by a vowel. Not all words ending with a ㅅ **s** conjugate this way; the exceptions must be memorized. Common words that do not lose their ㅅ **s** include 웃다 **utda** (to smile/laugh), 씻다 **ssitda** (to wash), and 벗다 **beotda** (to take off). An example of a word that does follow the irregular pattern is 낫다 **natda** (to be better). In front of the conjugation (ㄴ **n** / 은 **eun**), 낫다 **natda** loses its ㅅ **s** and becomes 나은 **naeun**. Below are more examples:

Korean (basic form)/ English	Present simple	Past	Future (will)	Past (adj.)	Future (adj.)
짓다 **jitda** (to build)	지어요 **jieoyo**	지었어요 **jieosseoyo**	짓겠어요 **jitgesseoyo**	지은 **jieun**	지을 **jieul**
긋다 **geutda** (to draw)	그어요 **geueoyo**	그었어요 **geueosseoyo**	긋겠어요 **geutgesseoyo**	그은 **geueun**	그을 **geueul**
붓다 **butda** (to pour)	부어요 **bueoyo**	부었어요 **bueosseoyo**	붓겠어요 **butgesseoyo**	부은 **bueun**	부을 **bueul**

ㅎ *h* **irregular verbs:** These verbs drop their ㅎ **h** when they are followed by a vowel. In 아 **a** / 어 **eo** conjugations, the vowel turns to ㅐ **ae**. An example of this is the verb 그렇다 **geureota** (to be so), which can be correctly conjugated by dropping the ㅎ **h** and adding ㅐ **ae**, to end up with 그래요 **geuraeyo**. More examples are found below:

Korean (basic form)/ English	Present simple	Past	Future (will)	Past (adj.)	Future (adj.)
어떻다 **eotteota** (how)	어때요 **eottaeyo**	어땠어요 **eottaesseoyo**	어떻겠어요 **eotteokesseoyo**	어떤 **eotteon**	어떨 **eotteol**
빨갛다 **ppalgata** (to be red)	빨개요 **ppalgaeyo**	빨갰어요 **ppalgaesseoyo**	빨갛겠어요 **ppalgakesseoyo**	빨간 **ppalgan**	빨갈 **ppalgal**

CULTURAL NOTE   **Eating While on the Move**

Korean people live very busy lives. They are constantly on the move, going to work, school, academies, and many other appointments. They continue to be busy all day and into the late night. Just walk into any street or subway station and you will see many Korean people hurrying from place to place. But just like other people, Koreans often eat on-the-go, and there are plenty of opportunities to grab a quick bite while en route.

Fortunately, there are lots of foods and beverages to buy along one's commute. In subway stations, travelers can purchase, from vending machines, a variety of snacks, drinks and hygiene products. In addition, many larger subway stations are replete with little shacks or chain restaurants selling a wide variety of foods—both Western and Korean. Furthermore, at both subway stations and bus stops—and pretty much any street corner—a hungry traveler can find a convenience store (편의점 **pyeonuijeom**) which is analogous to the inside portion of a gas station. For a very low price, you can purchase foods such as 삼각 김밥 **samgak gimbap** (a triangular-shaped rice and seaweed snack) or 도시락 **dosirak** (a microwaveable meal with rice, meat and sides).

Even when walking on the city streets between stops or stations, if you are looking for a bite to eat, you can stop at the many street vendors and tents selling delicious snacks. In a matter of seconds and for the value of just a couple of dollars, vendors will serve popular foods such as 떡볶이 **tteokbokki** (spicy and chewy rice cake), 오뎅 **odeng** (a fish-vegetable fried cake), 붕어빵 **bungeoppang** (a fish-shaped fried bread with cream or sweet red bean paste in the middle), 호떡 **hotteok** (a sweet, hot pancake filled with spices and brown sugar), or 타꼬야끼 **takkoyakki** (a Japanese-style ball-shaped bread, usually with chopped octopus in the middle).

However, visitors in South Korea should be cautious about eating while on the move. Many Koreans, especially the elder generation, consider eating while walking or talking to be poor-mannered. However, this expectation is changing with the younger generation.

Practice Activity 4

Decide whether the words below are regular or irregular verbs or adjectives.

1. 잇다 **itda** (to connect)
2. 먹다 **meokda** (to eat)
3. 아름답다 **areumdapda** (beautiful)
4. 내리다 **naerida** (to get off)
5. 다르다 **dareuda** (different)

Practice Activity 5

Practice conjugating the irregular verb, 돕다 **dopda** (to help) into the following forms:

1. present simple (-아요 / 어요 **ayo/eoyo**) _____

2. past (-았어요 / 었어요 **asseoyo/eosseoyo**) _____

3. future (-겠어요 **gesseoyo**) _____

4. past adjective (-ㄴ **n**)   _____

5. future adjective (-ㄹ / 을 **r / eul**)   _____

Practice Activity 6 Grammar review

1. Compare the characteristics of regular Korean verbs and adjectives with irregular verbs and adjectives.
2. Name six rules for irregular verbs and adjectives in Korean.

🎧 DIALOGUE 3 Tipping Customs

Anna learns about the no-tip policy in Korea from Jeonga.

Anna: Wow, this restaurant's food is really good.
         Wa, i sikdang eumsik jinjja masitda.
         와, 이 식당 음식 진짜 맛있다.

Jeonga: You are right. It was delicious.
         Maja. Jinjja masisseosseo.
         맞아. 진짜 맛있었어.

Anna: How much should we tip?
         Tibeun eolmana jwoya dwae?
         팁은 얼마나 줘야 돼?

Jeonga: There's no need to tip.
         Tibeun jul piryoeopseo.
         팁은 줄 필요없어.

Anna: Really? Is that allowed?
         Jeongmal? Geuraedo gwaenchana?
         정말? 그래도 괜찮아?

Jeonga: Yes. Tipping is Western culture. Koreans don't tip.
         Eung. Tibeun seoyang munhwaya. Hangugeseoneun tibeul an jwo.
         응. 팁은 서양 문화야. 한국에서는 팁을 안 줘.

Anna: I see, but I want to tip them.
         Geurae. Ne maeumeun jugo sipeunde.
         그래. 내 마음은 주고 싶은데…

Jeonga: Then, it's best to tell them it was a good meal.
         Geureomyeon, jal meogeotdago insahaneun ge jeil joa.
         그러면, 잘 먹었다고 인사하는 게 제일 좋아.

New Vocabulary 3

wow	와 **wa**
to give	주다 **juda**
no need	필요없다 **piryoeopda**
the West	서양 **seoyang**
if so	그러면 **geureomyeon**

GRAMMAR NOTE Expressing Possession (Part Two)

Expressing possession in Korean is surprisingly simple. As you learned in Lesson 8, as a general rule, adding the particle 의 **ui** after a person's name or object indicates that the person or object possesses the thing following it. Some examples are shown below:

이 책은 민호 씨의 책이다. **I chaegeun minho ssiui chaegida.**
This book is Minho's book.

나는 어제 친구의 집에 갔다. **Naneun eoje chinguui jibe gatda.**
Yesterday I went to a friend's house.

이 노래의 가사가 아주 좋아요. **I noraeui gasaga aju joayo.**
This song's lyrics are very good.

Using the particle 의 **ui** in this way to express possession will always result in a grammatically correct sentence. However, for a few commonly used words, Korean people prefer to use contractions to express possession and find these to be more natural. These contractions are 제 **je**, 내 **nae**, 네 **ne** (pronounced: 니 **ni**), 우리 **uri**, and 저희 **jeohi**. Below is a chart of the most commonly used words, how they contract, and how they can be used in a sentence:

Word	Standard	Contraction	Examples
저 **jeo** (I, me – polite form)	저의 **jeoui**	제 **je**	그분은 제 선생님입니다. **Geubuneun je seonsaengnimimnida.** *He is my teacher.*
나 **na** (I, me)	나의 **naui**	내 **nae**	너는 내 친구야. **Neoneun nae chinguya.** *You are my friend.*
너 **neo** (you)	너의 **neoui**	네 **ne**	이 빵은 네 거야. **I ppangeun ni kkeoya.** *This is your bread.*

Word	Standard	Contraction	Examples
우리 **uri** (we, us)	우리의 **uriui**	우리 **uri**	우리 집은 저쪽에 있어요 **Uri jibeun jeojjoge isseoyo.** *Our house is over there.*
저희 **jeohi** (we, us – polite form)	저희의 **jeohiui**	저희 **jeohi**	저희 차는 흰색입니다 **Jeohi chaneun huin saegimnida.** *Our car is white.*

It is important to note that Koreans use the contraction 우리 **uri** frequently to return to things that are not necessarily shared with anyone else. For example, a Korean woman might refer to her spouse as 우리 남편 **uri nampyeon** (our husband) or to Korea itself as 우리 나라 **uri nara** (our country). These usages do not indicate that a Korean person really thinks that you are married to the same husband or that you are a Korean citizen. Sometimes this style can simply be an affectionate way of showing respect or pride about the object it modifies. Feel free to match the style in order to share the same spirit of inclusiveness about relatives, mentors, organizations (such as church or work), or large possessions (cars, houses, etc.).

In addition, it is very important to be careful when describing something the speaker possesses. Koreans use the pronoun "you" very sparingly, and almost never use "you" in formal situations or when speaking to someone of higher status. In these circumstances, when Koreans want to refer to the speaker, they typically use the speaker's name or title or allow the speaker to infer through the context. However, using the low form of "you" is acceptable in casual situations among friends or those of lower rank, as demonstrated above with the possessive "너의" **neoui** contracting to "네" **ni**. Below are more examples demonstrating how to properly use possessive in specific situations:

PROPER:
우와, 네 차 진짜 멋있다. **Uwa, ni cha jinjja meositda.**
Wow, your car is super cool!

선생님의 차가 정말 멋있습니다.
Seonsaengnimui chaga jeongmal meositseumnida.
Your car is really cool!

미정 씨의 차가 되게 멋있네요. **Mijeong ssiui chaga doege meosinneyo.**
Wow, your [Mijeong's] car is very cool.

우리 차가 어제 고장 났어요. **Uri chaga eoje gojang nasseoyo.**
My [our] car broke down yesterday.

이 차는 우리 아버지의 동료의 차입니다.
I chaneun uri abeojiui dongnyoui chaimnida.
This car is my father's coworker's car.

IMPROPER:
우와, 당신의 차가 정말 멋있습니다.
Uwa, dangsinui chaga jeongmal meositseumnida.
Wow, your car is really cool.

The use of 당신 **dangsin** should generally be avoided.

CULTURAL NOTE   Korean versus Chinese Food

Both countries use rice, noodles, fresh vegetables, soy and meats liberally, but the sauces and flavors used in Korea are distinct. In particular, Korean cuisine tends to have stronger flavor resulting from liberal use of hot pepper paste or flakes (contributing a spicy taste) and fish sauce or Korean soybean paste (contributing a strong and deep salty taste, similar to Japanese miso). In addition, Koreans tend to eat more soups and stews than the Chinese, and as such spoons are much more prevalent at the dinner table in South Korea.

Korean and Chinese restaurants will look and feel different in other ways. In many restaurants that serve Korean food, meals are served at tables placed low to the ground and customers sit in the lotus position. Chinese meals in Korea are typically eaten while seated at Western-style tables. In addition, while the Chinese typically use round chopsticks made from wood, Koreans almost always use metal chopsticks with flat ends. Finally, whereas in Chinese cuisine the main dishes are the feature attraction of the dining experience, Korean meals are almost always served with 반찬 **banchan** (side dishes), such as kimchi, fish cake, or blanched sprouts or greens. Koreans love to achieve

a balance of colors, textures and flavors by alternating bites between the 반찬 **banchan** and the main course, and to many Koreans the number of 반찬 **banchan** available influences their perception of the fanciness of the meal or restaurant.

Koreans do not dislike Chinese food. In fact, one of the most beloved types of restaurants to Korean people and foreigners alike is the Korean Chinese restaurant. Although the food served at these restaurants is unique to Korea and cannot be found in China, the ingredients and cooking methods mimic those of Chinese recipes, adding a different base of flavoring that Korean people enjoy. It would be difficult to find a Korean Chinese restaurant that doesn't have 짜장면 **jjajangmyeon** or 짬뽕 **jjamppong**. 짜장면 **Jjajangmyeon** is a noodle dish served with chunks of meat and heaps of onion fried in a black, salty sauce, and is loved by foreigners and eaten almost weekly by Koreans. 짬뽕 **Jjamppong** uses the same kind of thick, boiled noodles, but presents these in a deep-red, spicy broth with other stir-fried vegetables and seafood. Both of these dishes are typically served with pickled radish and raw onion slices to dip in a salty, black paste.

Practice Activity 7

Match the English phrases with their equivalent Korean translations.

1. The teacher's book _____

2. My girlfriend _____

3. My house _____

4. Mother's food _____

5. My friend's restaurant _____

a. 내 집 **nae jip**

b. 내 친구의 음식점
   nae chinguui eumsikjeom

c. 어머니의 음식 **eomeoniui eumsik**

d. 내 여자친구 **nae yeojachingu**

e. 선생님의 책 **seonsaengnimui chaek**

🎧 Practice Activity 8

Listen to the cue below and respond. Then listen to the recorded response and repeat it.

1. Cue: 이것은 누구의 책이에요? **Igeoseun nuguui chaegieyo?**
   Whose book is this?
   Response: 이것은 제 책이에요. **Igeoseun je chaegieyo.** It's my book.

2. Cue: 저것은 누구의 여권이에요? **Jeogeoseun nuguui yeogwonieyo?**
    Whose passport is that?
    Response: 저것은 선생님의 여권이에요.
    Jeogeoseun seonsaengnimui yeogwonieyo.
    It's the teacher's passport.

* Repeat this drill substituting the list of words below.

1. 나 **na**, 우산 **usan**
2. 너 **neo**, 가방 **gabang**
3. 우리 **uri**, 엄마 **eomma**
4. 저 **jeo**, 노트북 **noteubuk**
5. 저희 **jeohi**, 집 **jip**

Practice Activity 9
Say the following in Korean using possessive markers.

1. My country's culture is different.
2. Jack's mom is a teacher.
3. Your car looks nice.
4. My friend's house is in Korea.

Taewoon, are you sick? Are you okay?

Taeun ssi, eodi apayo? Gwaenchaneuseyo?

Yes, I am okay. I am just a little tired.

Ne, gwaenchanayo. Geunyang jogeum pigonhaeyo.

Oh really? Did you study until late at night?

Geuraeyo? Bam neutgekkaji gongbuhasyeosseoyo?

Yes. I studied until 3 AM.

Ne. Saebyeok sesikkaji gongbuhaesseoyo.

Are you going to take a nap later?

Geureomyeon itta natjam jumusil geoyeyo?

I have finals today so I won't be able to nap.

Oneul ohue gimal siheomeul bwayo. Geuraeseo natjam mot jal geot gatayo.

LESSON 10
Expressing My Thoughts

🎧 ⌐ DIALOGUE 1 ┐ **I'm Feeling Tired.**

Peter notices Taeun looking tired and inquires further the reason.

Peter: Taewoon, are you sick? Are you okay?
          Taeun ssi, eodi apayo? Gwaenchaneuseyo?
          태운 씨, 어디 아파요? 괜찮으세요?

Taeun: Yes, I am okay. I am just a little tired.
          Ne, gwaenchanayo. Geunyang jogeum pigonhaeyo.
          네, 괜찮아요. 그냥 조금 피곤해요.

Peter: Oh really? Did you study until late at night?
          Geuraeyo? Bam neutgekkaji gongbuhasyeosseoyo?
          그래요? 밤 늦게까지 공부하셨어요?

Taeun: Yes. I studied until 3 AM.
          Ne. Saebyeok sesikkaji gongbuhaesseoyo.
          네. 새벽 3시까지 공부했어요.

Peter: Are you going to take a nap later?
          Geureomyeon itta natjam jumusil geoyeyo?
          그러면 이따 낮잠 주무실 거예요?

Taeun: I have finals today so I won't be able to nap.
          Oneul ohue gimal siheomeul bwayo. Geuraeseo natjam mot jal geot gatayo.
          오늘 오후에 기말 시험을 봐요. 그래서 낮잠 못 잘 것 같아요.

🎧 **New Vocabulary 1**

to be hurt, to be sick	아프다	**apeuda**
to be tired	피곤하다	**pigonhada**
to be late	늦다	**neutda**
night	밤	**bam**
to study	공부하다	**gongbuhada**
nap	낮잠	**natjam**
early morning/dawn	새벽	**saebyeok**
to sleep (honorific form)	주무시다	**jumusida**
later	이따	**itta**
afternoon	오후	**ohu**
final	기말	**gimal**
exam	시험	**siheom**
so	그래서	**geuraeseo**

GRAMMAR NOTE   Contracting Vowels

Did you notice in the previous conversation the conjugation of the verb 보다 **boda** (to see)? This is an example of vowel contraction, which is very common in Korean. To be formal, this verb would be conjugated 보아요 **boayo**, but for efficiency's sake, it is often shortened to 봐요 **bwayo**, especially in speech. Vowel contraction feels intuitive with experience, but for now you may reference general contraction rules below.

Identical vowel contraction

1. Situations where two identical vowels meet in a verb conjugation which cause the simplification of the vowels down to just one vowel.

   나 **na** + 아요 **ayo** = 나요 **nayo**   NOT 나아요 **naayo**
   가 **ga** + 아요 **ayo** = 가요 **gayo**   NOT 가아요 **gaayo**

2. Endings with 애 **ae** cancel out the following 어 **eo**:

   지내 **jinae** + 어요 **eoyo** = 지내요 **jinaeyo**   NOT 지내어요 **jinaeeoyo**

3. 이 **i** and 어 **eo** contract to become 여 **yeo**:

   가르치 **gareuchi** + 어요 **eoyo** = 가르쳐요 **gareuchyeoyo**
   기다리 **gidari** + 어요 **eoyo** = 기다려요 **gidaryeoyo**

There is an exception to 이 **i** becoming 여 **yeo**. When the honorific 시 **si** is used, it contracts to 세 **se**, not 셔 **syeo**.

   안녕하 **annyeongha** + 시 **si** + 어요 **eoyo** = 안녕하세요 **annyeonghaseyo**
   계시 **kyesi** + 어요 **eoyo** = 계세요 **kyeseyo**

Not every word that ends in 시 **si** is honorific. Words like 마시다 **masida** will still conjugate to 마셔요 **masyeoyo**.

4. 오 **o** and 우 **u** contract into diphthongs

   우 **u** + 어 **eo** = 워 **wo**
   오 **o** + 아 **a** = 와 **wa**

Contraction is optional when there is a consonant before the vowel, for example:

   주 **ju** + 어요 **eoyo** = 줘요 **jwoyo** or 주어요 **jueoyo**
   보 **bo** + 아요 **ayo** = 봐요 **bwayo** or 보아요 **boayo**

When there is no consonant before the vowel, contraction is not optional, for example:

오 **o** + 아요 **ayo** = 와요 **wayo**
배우 **baeu** + 어요 **eoyo** = 배워요 **baewoyo**

5. When words ending in 으 **eu** meet the syllable 어 **eo**, 으 **eu** is dropped and 어 **eo** is retained.

크 **keu** + 어요 **eoyo** = 커요 **keoyo**
쓰 **sseu** + 어요 **eoyo** = 써요 **sseoyo**

CULTURAL NOTE   What is 몸살 *momsal?*

After intense physical exercise, exposure to heat, or even mental exhaustion you may hear a Korean use the word 몸살 **momsal** to describe their physical condition. 몸살 **Momsal** is a word used to describe cold or fever-like symptoms which are due to bodily fatigue. You may hear it expressed as "몸살이 나다" **momsari nada**, an example sentence being "운동해서 몸살이 났다" **undonghaeseo momsari natda** (I exercised so much I got sick).

Practice Activity 1

Circle the correct contracted forms below.

1. 보아요 / 보어요

2. 해어요 / 해요

3. 내랴요 / 내려요

4. 드샤요 / 드셔요

5. 예빠요 / 예뻐요

Practice Activity 2

Go through the list below and conjugate them with -아요 / 어요 **ayo/eoyo** in a contracted form.

Words in unconjugated form	Contracted form
거짓말하다 **geojinmalhada** (to lie)	거짓말해요

1. 나가다 **nagada**   (to go out, leave) _____

2. 꿈꾸다 **kkumkkuda**   (to dream) _____

3. 도와주다 **dowajuda**   (to help) _____

4. 물어보다 **mureoboda**   (to ask) _____

5. 벗다 **beotda**   (to take off [clothes]) _____

6. 사다 **sada**   (to buy) _____

7. 서두르다 **seodureuda**   (to hurry) _____

8. 소개하다 **sogaehada**   (to introduce) _____

9. 오다 **oda** (to come) _____

10. 이기다 **igida** (to win) _____

11. 재다 **jaeda** (to measure, weigh) _____

12. 주다 **juda** (to give) _____

13. 지다 **jida** (to lose) _____

14. 하다 **hada** (to do) _____

15. 타다 **tada** (to ride) _____

Practice Activity 3

Repeat the dialogue (on page 143). See if you can pick out the verb and reverse its contraction to an unconjugated form.

1. 태운 씨, 어디 아파요? **Taeun ssi, eodi apayo?** Taewoon, are you sick?

   아파요 ➠ 아프다 _____

2. 괜찮으세요? **Gwaenchaneuseyo?** Are you okay?

   _____

3. 그냥 조금 피곤해요. **Geunyang jogeum pigonhaeyo.**
   I'm just a little tired.

   _____

4. 오늘 오후에 기말 시험을 봐요. **Oneul ohue gimal siheomeul bwayo.**
   This afternoon is the final exam.

   _____

5. 새벽 3시까지 공부했어요. **Saebyeok se(3)sikkaji gongbuhaesseoyo.**
   I studied until 3 AM. (dawn).

   _____

🎧 :DIALOGUE 2: **I'm Happy to Be Here.**

Junsuk finds out that it is the first time Peter is in Seoul.

Junsuk: Peter, is this your first visit to Seoul?
Piteo ssi, ibeoni Seoure cheoeum on geoyeyo?
피터 씨, 이번이 서울에 처음 온 거예요?

Peter: Yes. This is my first visit to Seoul, so I do not know Seoul well.
Ne. Cheoeum wasseoyo. Geuraeseo Seoure daehaeseo jal mollayo.
네. 처음 왔어요. 그래서 서울에 대해서 잘 몰라요.

Junsuk: Then shall we sightsee Seoul together? We can go to the baseball
          stadium, or go sightseeing at the Han River.
          **Geureomyeon gachi seoul gugyeongeul halkkayo? Yagujangdo gal
          su itgo hangangdo gal su isseoyo.**
          그러면 같이 서울 구경을 할까요? 야구장도 갈 수 있고 한강도 갈 수 있어요.

Peter: Wow, can we go to both? That would be really fun!
          Wa, dul da gal su isseoyo? Jinjja jaemiitgenneyo!
          와, 둘 다 갈 수 있어요? 진짜 재미있겠네요!

🎧 New Vocabulary 2

first	처음 **cheoeum**
to not know	모르다 **moreuda**
together	같이 **gachi**
sightseeing	구경 **gugyeong**
baseball stadium	야구장 **yagujang**
Han River	한강 **hangang**
both	둘 다 **dulda**

GRAMMAR NOTE   The Past Tense

Korean uses a few different conjugation forms in order to express actions in the past tense. Study the following example.

I saw a cat. 나는 고양이를 봤어요. **Naneun goyangireul bwasseoyo.**

Now take a look at what this same sentence would look like in the present tense.

I see a cat. 나는 고양이를 봐요. **Naneun goyangireul bwayo.**

Do you notice how the verb changed? When conjugating the past tense in Korean, begin by using the conjugation steps we learned in Lesson 4. First remove the 다 **da** from any verb or adjective. Then look at the word stem and find the last vowel. If the vowel is 아 **a** or 오 **o** then add 아 **a** and ㅆ **ss** to conjugate in the past tense. As you know, 아 **a** serves as a kind of "glue" that attaches the word stem to the conjugated ending. If you remove the 다 **da** and the final vowel is anything besides 아 **a** or 오 **oh** then add 어 **eo**. The only exception is verbs and adjectives that end in 하다 **hada**. The "glue" for those words is 해 **hae**. After you attach the "glue" just add the ㅆ **ss** and 어요 **eoyo** on the end to indicate the past tense. It looks like this:

보다 **boda** (base form) ➠ remove the 다 **da** ➠ ㅗ **o** corresponds with ㅏ **a**, so 보 **bo** + 아 **a** ➠ 봐 **bwa** through vowel contraction ➠ add the ㅆ **ss** to 봐 **bwa** ➠ 봤 **bwass** ➠ finish conjugating in your honorific level ➠ 봤어요 **bwasseoyo** (I saw).

This is a simple grammar form you will hear and use very frequently. Here are a few more examples so you can get a better idea of how this works.

Present Tense	Past Tense
나는 배워요.	나는 배웠어요.
Naneun baewoyo.	**Naneun baewosseoyo.**
I learn.	I learned.
그 남자는 마셔요.	그 남자는 마셨어요.
Geu namjaneun masyeoyo.	**Geu namjaneun masyeosseoyo.**
That man drinks.	That man drank.
우리는 행복해요.	우리는 행복했어요.
Urineun haengbokaeyo.	**Urineun haengbokaesseoyo.**
We are happy.	We were happy.

What if the verb you want to use in the past tense ends in a consonant? Remember to look past the last consonant and look at the last vowel so you know what "glue" to add. Here are some examples.

> 알다 **alda** ➠ 알았어요 **arasseoyo**
> (This is a common phrase used in the past tense to mean "I understand. I got it.")

> 걷다 **geotda** ➠ 걸었어요 **georeosseoyo**   I walked
> 읽다 **ikda** ➠ 읽었어요 **ilgeosseoyo**   I read
> 가지다 **gajida** ➠ 가졌어요 **gajyeosseoyo**   I have it or brought it

Notice how the 아 **a** and 어 **eo** stems do not merge with the verb behind it; they stand alone and the ㅆ **ss** is attached to the bottom of these stems, becoming 았 **at** and 었 **eot**.

🎧 **Practice Activity 4** Pronunciation

Practice saying the following words/phrases in Korean. Then listen to the audio to check your pronunciation.

1. 먹다 **meokda** / 먹었다 **meogeotda** / 먹었어요 **meogeosseoyo**
2. 자다 **jada** / 잤다 **jatda** / 잤어요 **jasseoyo**

3. 모르다 **moreuda** / 몰랐다 **mollatda** / 몰랐어요 **mollasseoyo**
4. 말하다 **malhada** / 말했다 **malhaetda** / 말했어요 **malhaesseoyo**
5. 이기다 **igida** / 이겼다 **igyeotda** / 이겼어요 **igyeosseoyo**

Practice Activity 5

Below is a list of commonly used verbs. Conjugate them into the past tense form and fill in the blanks on the right.

Present Tense	Past Tense
먹다 **meokda** (to eat)	_____
주다 **juda** (to give)	_____
만들다 **mandeulda** (to make)	_____
앉다 **anda** (to sit)	_____
일어나다 **ireonada** (to get up, rise)	_____
공부하다 **gongbuhada** (to study)	_____
기다리다 **gidarida** (to wait)	_____
대화하다 **daehwahada** (to talk)	_____
살다 **salda** (to live)	_____
보내다 **bonaeda** (to send)	_____
기억하다 **gieokada** (to remember)	_____
도착하다 **dochakada** (to arrive)	_____
끝나다 **kkeunnada** (to end)	_____
약속하다 **yaksokada** (to promise)	_____

🎧 **Practice Activity 6** Talk in Korean

Using some of the verbs you conjugated above, say the following sentences in Korean out loud. Words you may not yet know are in parenthesis next to their English translation.

1. I arrived in Seoul yesterday.
2. King Sejong (세종대왕 **sejongdaewang**) lived 600 years ago.
3. We had a talk yesterday.
4. I gave Mr. Lee my homework (숙제 **sukje**).
5. Did you eat kimchi?
6. Did you send a letter (편지 **pyeonji**) yesterday?

🎧 **DIALOGUE 3** I'm Very Busy.

Jihye finds out more about Joohyoung's job.

Jihye: Hello Jooyoung! Long time no see!
Juyeong ssi, annyeonghaseyo! Oraenmanineyo!
주영 씨, 안녕하세요! 오랜만이네요!

Jooyoung: Hello!
Annyeonghaseyo!
안녕하세요!

Jihye: What kind of work do you do these days?
Yojeum museun il haseyo?
요즘 무슨 일 하세요?

Jooyoung: I work at a trading company. It has been three months since I started working. I'm very busy.
Muyeok hoesae danyeoyo. Se(3)dal dwaesseoyo. Neomu bappayo.
무역 회사에 다녀요. 3달 됐어요. 너무 바빠요.

Jihye: Do you work on weekends?
Jumaredo ilhaseyo?
주말에도 일하세요?

Jooyoung: I work every Saturday. Sometimes I have to work from home on Sunday.
Ne. Toyoilmada ilhaeyo. Iryoiredo gakkeum jibeseo ilhaeyo.
네. 토요일마다 일해요. 일요일에도 가끔 집에서 일해요.

New Vocabulary 3

company	회사 **hoesa**
work	일 **il**
month	달 **dal**
to be busy	바쁘다 **bappeuda**
weekend	주말 **jumal**
Saturday	토요일 **toyoil**
every, each	마다 **mada**
Sunday	일요일 **iryoil**
sometimes	가끔 **gakkeum**

GRAMMAR NOTE   "What Kind of" vs "Which"

In Korean, there are two different words that can be confusing at first, since they can sometimes be interchangeable, and at other times they cannot. These words are 어느 **eoneu** and 무슨 **museun**. Both of these words precede nouns: 어느 **eoneu** + noun, 무슨 **museun** + noun.

어느 **Eoneu** is equivalent to the English word "which," so it brings a sense of specificity. You would not ask "which food do you like" to someone in English without providing or having an understanding of what can be chosen from. The same would go for the Korean usage. Let's take a look at a couple of examples in Korean.

어느 영화를 보고 싶어요? **Eoneu yeonghwareul bogo sipeoyo?**
Which movie do you want to see?

The word "which," in this case, is "connected" to the word 영화 **yeonghwa**. Keeping in mind the English example you studied a bit earlier, what does this sentence mean? Look at the correct and incorrect responses below.

CORRECT
"Lord of the Rings" 를 보고 싶어요. **"Lord of the Rings" reul bogo sipeoyo.**
I want to see Lord of the Rings.

INCORRECT
액션 영화를 보고 싶어요. **Aeksyeon yeonghwareul bogo sipeoyo.**
I want to see an action movie. (not specific enough).

Because the word 어느 **eoneu** carries with it a sense of specificity, you would answer or ask a question that requires a specific answer. Even in English if someone were to ask the above question and answer with "I want to see an action movie" it would sound awkward. It works the same way in Korean.

In the conversation above, Jihye asks Jooyoung what kind of work she is doing by using 무슨 **museun** because 무슨 **museun** has a more vague meaning. It would be awkward if Jihye used 어느 **eoneu** here. In English, if you ask "What food do you like" it can refer to any type of food, not anything specific. This is the same in Korean. See the example below.

무슨 음식을 좋아해요? **Museun eumsigeul joahaeyo?**
What food do you like?

Now that you have learned what 어느 **eoneu** and 무슨 **museun** mean, look at the sentences below to see which ones are correct responses to the above question.

CORRECT
한국 음식을 좋아해요. **Hanguk eumsigeul joahaeyo.**
I like Korean food.

CORRECT
매운 음식을 좋아해요. **Maeun eumsigeul joahaeyo.**
I like spicy food.

INCORRECT
비빔밥을 좋아해요. **Bibimbabeul joahaeyo.**
I like bibimbap.

Since the question was asked with 무슨 **museun** a more general answer is given. A more specific answer may not be technically incorrect, but is awkward to Korean ears.

CULTURAL NOTE **The "Face" Issue**

As you travel in Korea, you will start to get an understanding of how korean society functions. There is a sort of "social hierarchy" to Korean society, determined by factors like age, sex, seniority, prestige, and rank. For example, the Korean word for "friend" is 친구 **chingu**. However, this word is reserved for people who are the same age as you. There are many other relationships with their own relational terms (as you may recall from Lesson 5). These relationships are important in Korean society, and outsiders may need time to become familiar with them.

It's important to understand that in Korea "face" does not refer to just a person's physical features. "Face" can refer to reputation, social standing, dignity, influence, or honor, among other things. Through interactions on a daily basis, people can "lose face" and "save (or gain) face." Causing someone personal embarrassment in public would cause them to lose face, even if no harm was intended.

Imagine walking down the street and you see someone with one pant leg tucked accidentally into their sock. In some countries, it would be appreciated and even funny to point it out so they could take care of it, and both parties would go on their way. In Korea, to point this out would cause the person embarrassment, and thus they would "lose face." In many cases, the best solution would be to ignore the situation. If everyone pretends they don't see, and the person is able to take care of it in private, that person will have avoided losing face.

On the other hand, you can gain face and give face. Humility plays a big role in this. Imagine you win a prize at the science fair. In some countries you would most likely accept the reward and even be proud of yourself. In Korea doing that would cause you to lose face. To gain and give face, you would act humbly when receiving the reward, perhaps saying that you don't deserve it—it should go to your teacher, who helped you work on it for hours, or the classmate who gave you helpful tips. In this case you would be gaining face by being humble, and giving face by giving credit to those who helped you. It's a win-win situation!

Keep in mind that this has been a part of Korean culture for a very long time. Koreans can read these situations well, and a disingenuous response or action could cause you to lose face as well!

Practice Activity 7

Practice saying the following English sentences in Korean using the right word: 어느 **eoneu** or 무슨 **museun**. Then use the audio to check your answers and pronunciation.

1. What music do you like?

2. Which song do you like?

3. What type of book do you usually read?

4. Which book do you like the most?

5. Which country do you want to go to?

Practice Activity 8 **Role-Play**

1. You are dating someone. Ask him/her what kind of music he/she likes.
2. Ask a salesman what the best-selling car in the store is.
3. Ask your friend from which country he/she came from.
4. You are at a movie theater. Ask your friend which movie to see.
5. Find out what kind of job Minhee wants to have in the future.

Oh. Are you going to marry him?

Geureokunyo. Namja chingurang gyeolhonhasil geoyeyo?

Sehui, thank you for everything today. Wasn't it difficult to prepare for the party?

Sehui ssi, oneul jeongmal gamsahamnida. Pati junbihaneura himdeulji aneusyeosseoyo?

No. My boyfriend helped me a lot.

Aniyo. Namja chinguga dowa-jwoseo gwaenchanasseoyo.

~nom~

I'm not sure about that.

Jal moreugesseoyo.

I see. Do you want some leftover *jumeokbap*?

Ne. Yeogi nameun jumeokbap an deusillaeyo?

Right now my stomach is so full. I'll eat it later.

A, ne. Jigeum baega neomu bulleoyo. Najunge meogeulgeyo.

Abiding by Social Etiquette

🎧 | DIALOGUE 1 | **Thanks for Everything!**

Emma has a conversation with Sehui after a recent party.

Emma: Sehui, thank you for everything today. Wasn't it difficult to prepare for the party?
Sehui ssi, oneul jeongmal gamsahamnida. Pati junbihaneura himdeulji aneusyeosseoyo?
세희 씨, 오늘 정말 감사합니다. 파티 준비하느라 힘들지 않으셨어요?

Sehui: No. My boyfriend helped me a lot.
Aniyo. Namja chinguga dowajwoseo gwaenchanasseoyo.
아니요. 남자 친구가 도와줘서 괜찮았어요.

Emma: Oh. Are you going to marry him?
Geureokunyo. Namja chingurang gyeolhonhasil geoyeyo?
그렇군요. 남자 친구랑 결혼하실 거예요?

Sehui: I'm not sure about that.
Jal moreugesseoyo.
잘 모르겠어요.

Emma: I see. Do you want some leftover *jumeokbap*?
Ne. Yeogi nameun jumeokbap an deusillaeyo?
네. 여기 남은 주먹밥 안 드실래요?

Sehui: Right now my stomach is so full. I'll eat it later.
A, ne. Jigeum baega neomu bulleoyo. Najunge meogeulgeyo.
아, 네. 지금 배가 너무 불러요. 나중에 먹을게요.

🎧 **New Vocabulary 1**

thankful	감사하다	gamsahada
to be straining/exhausting	힘들다	himdeulda
to not be	않다	anta
I see, so	그렇군요	geureokunyo
to marry	결혼하다	gyeolhonhada
rice balls	주먹밥	jumeokbap
to be full	부르다	bureuda
later	나중	najung

GRAMMAR NOTE   Forming Negative Questions

In Korean there are a few ways to make verbs negative. We learned a couple of ways in Lesson 8 and we will add to that discussion here. As you know, the first method is by adding 안 **an** in front of the verb. Another way is by adding 지 **ji** + 않다 **anta** to the verb stem (drop the "다" **da** to get the verb stem). Let's look at some examples.

Base Verb	안 an + Verb	Verb Stem + 지 않다
먹다 **meokda** to eat	안 먹다 **an meokda**	먹지 않다 **meokji anta**
가다 **gada** to go	안 가다 **an gada**	가지 않다 **gaji anta**
하다 **hada** to do	안 하다 **an hada**	하지 않다 **haji anta**

드시다 **Deusida** is an honorific form of 먹다 **meokda** (to eat). You are honoring the person who is eating. Emma made it negative by saying "안 드시다" **an deusida** (you aren't eating?) and conjugated it to polite 요 **yo** form. To be more polite, it's good to end all questions about someone's intention with 세요 **seyo**. Emma also asked a negative past tense question. While 먹다 **meokda** has a specific honorific form, the verb 않다 **anta** (to not be) does not. To make it honorific, add (으)시 **(eu)si** to the verb stem. The new verb is 않으시다 **aneusida**. Then Emma asked in the past tense, "힘들지 않으셨어요?" **Himdeulji aneusyeosseoyo?** (Wasn't it difficult?).

As you may remember from Lesson 8, in English when someone is asked a negative question and confirms the negativity, the person responds with a negative answer such as, "You're not going?" "No, I'm not." In Korean, however, you respond with a positive answer when confirming a negative question. "안가요?" **Angayo?** (You aren't going?), "네, 안가요." **Ne, angayo.** (Yes, I'm not going). This only applies to negative questions.

One limitation of the Korean negative form is that 안 **an** + verb cannot be used directly in front of nouns (though it can be used with 하다 **hada** itself).

CORRECT
식사 안 하세요? **Siksa an haseyo?**
Are you not going to have a meal?

INCORRECT
안 식사하세요? **An sikahaseyo?**
Are you not going to have a meal?

CULTURAL NOTE   Ways to Express Thanks

In Korea, manners (예 **ye** or 예의 **yeui**) are very important. Korea is traditionally a Confucian society and Koreans typically try to be careful to show respect for those older than themselves. Naturally expressing thanks is also an important aspect of this respectful culture. In Korean language there are various ways to conjugate verbs to make the sentence polite, formal, and/or honorific. As you saw above, the honorific form of 먹다 **meokda** is 드시다 **deusida**. There are seven main verbs which have a distinct, separate word for the honorific form. These are all very common words so you'll learn them quickly.

Normal	Honorific
먹다 **meokda** to eat	드시다 **deusida**
자다 **jada** to sleep	주무시다 **jumusida**
있다 **itda** to exist	계시다 **gyesida**
주다 **juda** to give	드리다 **deurida**
만나다 **mannada** to meet	뵙다 **boepda**
말하다 **malhada** to say, speak	말씀하시다 **malsseumhasida**
묻다 **mutda** to ask	여쭤보다 **yeojjwoboda**

The rest of the time we make verbs honorific by adding (으)시 (**eu**)**si** to the verb stem. Here are some examples.

Normal	Honorific
앉다 **anda** to sit	앉으시다 **anjeusida**
이다 **ida** to be	이시다 **isida**
다니다 **danida** to attend	다니시다 **danisida**
살다 **salda** to live	사시다 **sasida**
걷다 **geotda** to walk	걸으시다 **georeusida**

There are always exceptions, as you learned in Lesson 9. In verbs that have a ㄹ **r** before the 다 **da**, we drop the ㄹ **r**. And in verbs that have a ㄷ **d** before the 다 **da** we change it into a ㄹ **r**.

There are also honorific versions of some nouns. These are the most common:

Normal	Honorific
사람 **saram** person	분 **bun**
이름 **ireum** name	성함 **seongham**
아내 **anae** wife	부인 **buin**
집 **jip** house	댁 **daek**
나이 **nai** age	연세 **yeonse**
생일 **saengnil** birthday	생신 **saengsin**
형 **hyeong** / 누나 **nuna** brother/sister	형님 / 누님 **hyeongnim/nunim**
딸 **ttal** / 아들 **adeul** daughter/son	따님 / 아드님 **ttanim/adeunim**
할머니 **halmeoni** / 할아버지 **harabeoji** grandmother/grandfather	할머님 **halmeonim** / 할아버님 **harabeonim**
아버지 **abeoji** / 어머니 **eomeoni** father/mother	아버님 **abeonim** / 어머님 **eomeonim**

You can see from the chart that when it comes to people's titles the way to honor them is by adding "님" **nim**. This is all part of the Korean culture of respect. It's important to review that for people older than you, you should refer to them by their name + title or just their title. Never refer to them by just their name.

Practice Activity 1

Change each of the following words to the "aren't you?" (negative) forms with the honorific marker "세" **se**. Be sure not to use the honorific marker when there is a matching honorific form (e.g., 안 먹어요 [O], 안 먹으세요 [X]).

Korean	"Aren't you?" Forms
Examples	
하다 **hada** (to do)	안 하세요? / 하지 않으세요?
먹다 **meokda** (to eat)	_____
드시다 **deusida** (to eat [honorific])	_____
결혼하다 **gyeolhonhada** (to get married)	_____
자다 **jada** (to sleep)	_____
주무시다 **jumusida** (to sleep [honorific])	_____

Korean	"Aren't you?" Forms
사용하다 **sayonghada** (to use)	_____

🎧 Practice Activity 2

Read the questions and respond with a positive answer if you agree with the question, or with a negative answer if you disagree with the question.

1. Cue: 아침 안 먹어요? **Achim an meogeoyo?**
   Are you not going to have breakfast?

   Answer: _____ , 안 먹어요.   _____ , **an meogeoyo.**
   Yes, I'm not eating.

2. Cue: 안 잘 거예요? **An jal geoyeyo?**
   Are you not going to sleep?

   Answer: _____ , 안 자요.   _____ , **an jayo.**
   Yes, I'm not going to sleep.

3. Cue: 결혼 안 할 거예요? **Gyeolhon an hal geoyeyo?**
   Are you not going to get married?

   Answer: _____ , 할 거예요.   _____ , **hal geoyeyo.**
   No, I'm going to get married.

4. Cue: 숙제 안 할 거예요? **Sukje an hal geoyeyo?**
   Are you not going to do your homework?

   Answer: _____ , 숙제 할 거예요.   _____ , **Sukje hal geoyeyo.**
   No, I'm going to do my homework.

5. Cue: 할아버지가 이 집에 안 사세요? **Harabeojiga i jibe an saseyo?**
   Is your grandfather not living in this house?

   Answer: _____ , 다른 집에 사세요.   _____ , **dareun jibe saseyo.**
   Yes, he is living in another house.

🎧 : DIALOGUE 2 : **Saying Goodbye to Friends**

Joseph and Jonghun part ways after a night out.

Joseph: Jonghun, it was fun hanging out with you.
            Jonghuni hyeong, oneul deokbune jaemiisseosseoyo.
            종훈이 형, 오늘 덕분에 재미있었어요.

Jonghun: Yes, me too. How are you getting home? It's late.
            Geurae. Nado jaemiisseotda. Neo, neujeonneunde jibe eotteoke gani?
            그래. 나도 재미있었다. 너, 늦었는데 집에 어떻게 가니?

Joseph: I'm going to grab a taxi.
            Jeoneun taeksitago galgeyo.
            저는 택시타고 갈게요.

Jonghun: All right. Take care.
            Geurae. Josimhaeseo deureogara.
            그래. 조심해서 들어가라.

Joseph: See you tomorrow.
            Ne. Naeil boeyo.
            네. 내일 뵈요.

Jonghun: Oh, tomorrow doesn't work for me. Maybe next week?
            A. Naeireun naega jom eoryeopgo. Daeumjue boja?
            아. 내일은 내가 좀 어렵고. 다음주에 보자?

Joseph: Sounds good. Take care.
            Ne, geuraeyo. Josimhaeseo deureogaseyo.
            네, 그래요. 조심해서 들어가세요.

🎧   New Vocabulary 2

thanks to	덕분에	**deokbune**
to be careful	조심하다	**josimhada**
to go in	들어가다	**deureogada**
hard to do	어렵다	**eoryeopda**

In the above conversation, Joseph calls Jonghun by the title "형" **hyeong** meaning older brother. Although they are close with each other, it is still correct for younger men to call older men 형 **hyeong**. Jonghun uses casual speech (반말 **banmal**) which is characterized by short endings with no "요" **yo** or "습니다" **seumnida**. Joseph meanwhile uses the polite 요 **yo** ending as a sign of respect for his elder. When there is little age difference, the older person in a close relationship may ask the younger to drop the 요 **yo** and just speak casually.

GRAMMAR NOTE The Deferential Mood

In formal situations in Korea the deferential mood is used. Formal situations include, but are not limited to, business meetings and office interactions, public speeches, meetings with mentors or leaders, meetings with political figures, meetings with those much older than you, among military personnel, when making an announcement, or speaking to customers, etc. As you can see this speech form is useful when speaking to anyone who you defer to or whose service you are employed in.

Deferential mood is expressed using 습니다 **seumnida**. This is a type of verb conjugation characterized by adding the ㅂ니다 **b nida** / 습니다 **seumnida** ending. The deferential form is a type of 존댓말 **jondaenmal** (polite speech which also includes polite speech ending in 요 **yo**).

Conjugation for the deferential ㅂ니다 **b nida** / 습니다 **seumnida** ending is extremely simple. Simply drop the 다 **da** off of the infinitive form, or dictionary form of the verb, and add ㅂ니다 **b nida** for verb stems ending in a vowel, and 습니다 **seumnida** for verb stems ending in a consonant.

Base Verb	Verb Stem	Present Tense Verb
먹다 **meokda** to eat	먹- **meok-**	먹습니다 **meokseumnida**
가다 **gada** to go	가- **ga-**	갑니다 **gamnida**
살다 **salda** to live	살- **sal-**	삽니다 **samnida**
하다 **hada** to do	하- **ha-**	합니다 **hamnida**
듣다 **deutda** to listen	듣- **deut-**	듣습니다 **deutseumnida**

Notice there is an exception to this rule. For verb stems ending in "ㄹ" **r**, the ㅂ니다 **b nida** ending is used, not 습니다 **seumnida**.

Now let's look at the past and future tense.

Base Verb	Past tense	Past–tense verb stem	Past tense
먹다 **meokda**	먹었다 **meogeotda**	먹었- **meogeot-**	먹었습니다 **meogeotseumnida**
가다 **gada**	갔다 **gatda**	갔- **gat-**	갔습니다 **gatseumnida**
살다 **salda**	살았다 **saratda**	살았- **sarat-**	살았습니다 **saratseumnida**
하다 **hada**	했다 **haetda**	했- **haet-**	했습니다 **haetseumnida**
듣다 **deutda**	들었다 **deureotda**	들었- **deureot-**	들었습니다 **deureotseumnida**

Base Verb	Future tense	Future-tense verb stem	Future tense
먹다 meokda	먹었다 meogeotda	먹겠- meokget-	먹겠습니다 meokgetseumnida
가다 gada	가겠다 gagetda	가겠- gaget-	가겠습니다 gagetseumnida
살다 salda	살겠다 salgetda	살겠- salget-	살겠습니다 salgetseumnida
하다 hada	하겠다 hagetda	하겠- haget-	하겠습니다 hagetseumnida
듣다 deutda	듣겠다 deutgetda	듣겠- deutget-	듣겠습니다 deutgetseumnida

In deferential form, you can make any statement a question by changing the 다 da to a 까 kka.

Statement	Question
먹었습니다 meogeotseumnida	먹었습니까 Meogeotseumnikka? *Did you eat?*
갔습니다 gatseumnida	갔습니까 Gatseumnikka? *Did you go?*

Practice Activity 3

Conjugate the words to honorific form using deferential endings with tense markers.

Words	Present tense	Present tense – question	Past tense	Future tense
공부하다 gongbuhada				
듣다 deutda				
생각하다 saenggakada				
연락하다 yeollakada				
두다 duda				

CULTURAL NOTE   Interacting with Others in the Workplace

Koreans are known for working long hours. In Korea employees are often reluctant to leave the office before their boss because they don't want to appear to be slacking off. Additionally, it's common for employees to bond over frequent work dinners, known as 회식 **hoesik,** where the socializing and drinking culture mix with the work culture. Although not mandatory, if you choose not to attend work dinners, you may be seen as an outsider. There is often beer and soju (Korean-made alcoholic drink similar to vodka) served at 회식. If you prefer not to drink, politely inform your superiors and you will likely be served a soda. Recently there have been movements within Korea against the excessive work-dinner culture which results in very long workdays and poses health risks from heavy drinking. However, because of the time spent together in various settings and because of the deep bonds they form with their co-workers, it's rare for Koreans to switch jobs frequently.

In addition, if you plan to work in Korea, it might be beneficial to understand appropriate interaction between employees and supervisors. In many western cultures, the employee generally stays at their desk or workstation, and their manager or supervisor is often the one who inquires about progress on a project, etc. In Korea the responsibility is on you to report progress to your boss.

As we have already discussed in this book, bowing is the appropriate greeting in Korea. It's also important to know that in Korea the person who has a lower social status should introduce themselves to the person with higher social status, first. This is especially true in the workplace. Typically, it's best to shake hands only when a hand is offered to you. Remember to shake with your right hand and keep your left hand touching your right arm at about your elbow. Koreans value hard work, and if you prove yourself, you will gain acceptance in the company and make many lifelong friends.

🎧 Practice Activity 4

Say the following statements and questions in Korean using the deferential ending plus past and future tense, if needed. Then listen to the audio to check your answers and pronunciation.

1. Do you live in Korea?
2. I live in the United States.
3. I will go to school tomorrow.
4. I will listen to music this afternoon.
5. I do my homework every day.
6. I will help my mom.
7. The exam was hard.

Practice Activity 5

Conjugate the following verbs into their correct deferential tone as a junior chef speaks to his head chef.

> **Word Bank**
>
> 이다 **ida** to be
> 끝내다 **kkeunnaeda** to finish
> 있다 **itda** to exist
> 알다 **alda** to know

Head Chef: Are you doing what I told you to do?
내가 말한대로 하고 있어? **Naega malhandaero hago isseo?**

Junior Chef: Yes, I am doing as you've asked.
네, 하고 _____. **Nae, hago _____.**

Head Chef: Did you finish cleaning?
청소 끝냈어? **Cheongso kkeunnaesseo?**

Junior Chef: Yes, Chef, I finished cleaning.
네 셰프님, _____. **Ne syepeunim, _____.**

Head Chef: What about preparing the vegetables?
야채 준비는? **Yachae junbineun?**

Junior Chef: I'm still working on it.
아직 준비 중 _____. **Ajik junbi jung _____.**

Head Chef: Hurry up.
빨리 해. **Ppalli hae.**

Junior Chef: Yes, I will.
네, _____. **Ne, _____.**

*Note: In the last example 알다 **alda** should be conjugated to 알겠습니다 **algetseumnida**. Using the past tense 알았습니다 **aratseumnida** or the present tense 압니다 **amnida** can sound presumptuous. It is more polite to use 겠 **get** to express your willingness in this context.

🎧 **DIALOGUE 3 Buying a Gift**

Yunji and Jeongbin go shopping for a present.

Yunji: Would Miran like this?
Miraniga igeo joahalkka?
미란이가 이거 좋아할까?

Jeongbin: What is it? Show me.
Mwonde? Boyeojwo bwa.
뭔데? 보여줘 봐.

Yunji: It's this perfume. What do you think?
Eung. Igeo hyangsuinde, eottae?
응. 이거 향수인데, 어때?

Jeongbin: Miran doesn't like those kinds of perfumes.
Miranineun geureon hyangsu an joahae.
미란이는 그런 향수 안 좋아해.

Yunji: Oh, really? Then, what should we buy for her?
Geurae? Geureom mwoga joeulkka?
그래? 그럼 뭐가 좋을까?

Jeongbin: Um. I think that makeup would be a better birthday gift for her.
Eum, saengnil seonmulloneun jeoreon hwajangpumi deo naa.
음, 생일 선물로는 저런 화장품이 더 나아.

Yunji: Ok. Then let's buy makeup.
Geureokuna. Geureom hwajangpumeul saja.
그렇구나. 그럼 화장품을 사자.

🎧 **New Vocabulary 3**

to show	보여주다	boyeojuda
perfume	향수	hyangsu
makeup	화장품	hwajangpum
to be better	낫다	natda
to buy	사다	sada

GRAMMAR NOTE Demonstrative Pronouns

Demonstratives are important words that help us navigate the world around us. Demonstratives indicate the relative relationship between things, helping us determine direction, location, size, distance, time, and more. English demonstratives include words like "this," "that," "these," and "those," which are also pronouns. Korean demonstratives function the same way and follow an extremely logical pattern. This is called the "이 i – 그 geu – 저 jeo – 어 eo" pattern.

이 i	this
그 geu	that
저 jeo	that (over there)
어느 eoneu	which

Something interesting about English demonstratives is that they can function as a noun or an adjective depending on the context. (For example: "This is unacceptable," "This car is nice.") The words we have just learned are adjectives only. They modify other words, for example:

이 사람 i saram	this person
그 말 geu mal	those words
저 나무 jeo namu	that tree (over there)
어느 나라 eoneu nara	which country

In English, a distinction is only made between things that are directly in front of the speaker, and things that are not. In Korean a distinction is made between things near the speaker (이 i), things near the listener (그 geu), and things near neither the speaker nor the listener (저 jeo).

If you want to convert these adjectives into nouns you can add the general word for "thing."

이것 igeot	this thing
그것 geugeot	that thing
저것 jeogeot	that thing (over there)
어느 것 eoneu geot	which thing

Notice that there is no space when you use "것" geot except 어느 eoneu. Let's look at some more demonstrative words that follow this 이 i – 그 geu – 저 jeo – 어 eo pattern.

여기 **yeogi**	here
거기 **geogi**	there
저기 **jeogi**	(over) there
어디 **eodi**	where

Location words follow the pattern closely (except 이 **i** becomes 여 **yeo**, and 그 **geu** becomes 거 **geo**). Importantly, these words are nouns, not adjectives, meaning they can stand on their own.

이런 **ireon**	this kind
그런 **geureon**	that kind
저런 **jeoreon**	that kind
어떤 **eotteon**	which kind

The difference between 그런 **geureon** and 저런 **jeoreon** is more subtle since we're not talking about physical distance. 저런 **Jeoreon** is used when the topic being modified is in sight or has just been seen so the listener knows who or what is being referred to. 그런 **Geureon** is used for a topic that is not in the place where a conversation is held (e.g., someone who is somewhere else) or that is abstract/invisible (e.g., thoughts, ideas, government policy, or characteristics of a person). The same words in adverbial form are listed below.

이렇게 **ireoke**	this way
그렇게 **geureoke**	that way
저렇게 **jeoreoke**	that way
어떻게 **eotteoke**	how/in which way

Finally, 만큼 **mankeum** means "amount" and is a dependent noun. There are many more common examples utilizing this 이 **i** – 그 **geu** – 저 **jeo** – 어 **eo** pattern, but this will suffice for now.

이 만큼 **i mankeum**	this much
그 만큼 **geu mankeum**	that much
저 만큼 **jeo mankeum**	that much
얼만큼 **eolmankeum**	how much

CULTURAL NOTE   Giving and Accepting Gifts

Giving gifts at appropriate times is an important part of Korean culture. While there are few cases where a gift is a must, gifts definitely go a long way when given thoughtfully. Typically, if you are invited to stay at someone's house, a gift is an appropriate show of appreciation. In this scenario, a food gift basket or household items (such as wet wipes, utensils, dining ware, etc.) are appropriate. If you are coming from far away, a gift representative of your hometown is always good. Koreans appreciate things that are useful or things that can be displayed as a sign of status.

In a romantic relationship, gift giving may be similar to western gift giving. However, if a Korean gives a gift, it is typical for them to expect an equally thoughtful gift in return. In Korean society there is an understood culture of taking turns in paying for the other's meals and giving gifts (though this may vary if there is a significant age gap). On birthdays you may treat your friend or significant other to a meal or give them new clothes or skin care products. Cosmetic items are a great go-to in Korea.

In Korean families it's typical for children to receive some spending money (known as 세뱃돈 **sebaetdon**) as a gift during the Lunar New Year holiday (known as 설날 **seollal** in Korea). If you are young (have not reached working age), you may find yourself on the receiving end of this, and if you are older you may consider giving money to any young people you share the holiday with. Before receiving money, the younger person bows to the older person. Typically, this gift is most commonly given by grandparents to grandchildren, but other family members or family friends often give as well.

Finally, sharing food is ingrained in Korean society. It's very neighborly to share side dishes, extra fruit or vegetables (perhaps things you've picked out of your garden), and most classically kimchi. Kimchi is made every year in the fall (and often throughout the year), and it's great to share kimchi flavors with your neighbor (assuming you live in an individual home or family apartment). If you do this, you may expect something delicious in return.

Practice Activity 6

Read the English phrases and fill in the blanks with equivalent Korean demonstrative pronouns.

1. I've never seen a person who is that nice.

   _____ 친절한 사람은 처음이에요.

   _____ **chinjeolhan sarameun cheoeumieyo.**

2. How difficult is Korean?

   한국어가 _____ 어려워요?

   Hangugeoga _____ **eoryeowoyo?**

3. How did you come to Korea?

   _____ 한국에 왔어요?

   _____ **hanguge wasseoyo?**

4. I'd like to visit this kind of place again.

   _____ 곳에 또 오고 싶어요.

   _____ **gose tto ogo sipeoyo.**

5. That person is Mr. Kim Young Cheol.

   _____ 사람이 김영철 씨예요.

   _____ **sarami Gimyeongcheol ssiyeyo.**

🎧 Practice Activity 7

The dialogues below are sample exchanges using demonstrative pronouns. In pairs, try to guess the location of the speaker, the listener and any objects in the conversation. Listen to the audio and repeat each line aloud.

1.   A: 거기로 갈까요? **Geogiro galkkayo?**
        Shall I go there?

     B: 네. 이리로 오세요 **Ne. Iriro oseyo.**
        Yes. Come over here.

2.   A: 이것을 사세요. **Igeoseul saseyo.**
        Buy this one.

     B: 그것은 너무 비싸요. **Geugeoseun neomu bissayo.**
        That one is too expensive.

3.   A: 얼만큼 살까요? **Eolmankeum salkkayo?**
        How much should I buy?

     B: 이 만큼 사면 돼요. **I mankeum samyeon dwaeyo.**
        This much is enough.

4.   A: 저렇게 하면 돼요? **Jeoreoke hamyeon dwaeyo?**
        Should I do it that way?

     B: 아니요. 이렇게 하세요. **Aniyo. Ireoke haseyo.**
        No. Do it this way.

5.   A: 이런 식당이 또 있어요? **Ireon sikdangi tto isseoyo?**
        Is there another restaurant like this?

     B: 네. 저쪽에 비슷한 식당이 많아요. **Ne. Jeojjoge biseutan sikdangi manayo.**
        Yes, there are similar restaurants over there.

Practice Activity 8

Mark the appropriate reference point for each pronoun. Some pronouns may have more than one match.

	이것	저것	그것	어느 것
Far from both speaker and listener				
Far from speaker and close to listener				
Close to speaker and far from listener				
Close to both speaker and listener				
Abstract object				
Which				

Answer Key to Exercises

LESSON 1
Practice Activity 2
1. I'm sorry (formal)　　2. Thank you　　3. Excuse me　　4. Perhaps

Practice Activity 3
Example:
서울역은 어디에 있어요?
홍대는 어디에 있어요?
제주도는 어디에 있어요?

LESSON 2
Practice Activity 1
Examples:
피자 주세요.
반지 있어요?
콜라 있어요?

Practice Activity 2
쇼핑 센터가 어디 있어요?
시장이 어디 있어요?
서점이 어디 있어요?
빵집이 어디 있어요?

Answer for Crossword Puzzle (p 36)

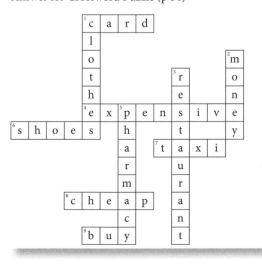

Across
1. 카드 (card)
4. 비싸다 (expensive)
6. 신발 (shoes)
7. 택시 (taxi)
8. 싸다 (cheap)
9. 사다 (buy)

Down
1. 옷 (clothes)
2. 돈 (money)
3. 식당 (resturant)
5. 약국 (pharmacy)

Practice Activity 3

1. I want to buy a camera.   2. Do you have money?   3. Please give me pizza.
   카메라 사고 싶어요.   돈 있어요?   피자 주세요.

LESSON 3
Practice Activity 1

1. 는   2. 은   3. 는   4. 는   5. 는

Practice Activity 2

1. 왔어요   2. 한국   3. 안가요   4. 안다니고 있어요

Practice Activity 3

1. 않아요   2. 않아요   3. 못   4. 못   5. 못/안

LESSON 4
Practice Activity 1

1. 도, 에   2. 도, 를   3. 도, 를   4. 도, 를   5. 에도, 가

Practice Activity 2

1. 는   2. 은   3. 은   4. 는

Practice Activity 3

1. 먹어요   2. 타요   3. 가요   4. 감아요   5. 내려요

LESSON 5
Practice Activity 1

1. 괜찮다   → b. 괜찮은
2. 있다   → g. 있는
3. 없다   → c. 없는
4. 쉽다   → f. 쉬운
5. 중요하다 → e. 중요한
6. 알다   → d. 아는
7. 좋다   → a. 좋은

Practice Activity 2

1. 오는 길   2. 주문한 파스타   3. 중요한 시험   4. 반가운 친구
5. 재미있는 영화

Practice Activity 3

1. 남동생   2. Younger sister   3. 선배   4. 몇   5. Older brother
6. Older sister

Practice Activity 4

1. 집   → c. home
2. 신발   → b. shoes
3. 초대하다 → d. to invite

4. 신발장   → e. shoe closet
5. 온돌   → f. underfloor heating system
6. 없다   → a. not exist

Practice Activity 5
1. 이, 있어요   2. 가, 없어요   3. 이, 있어요   4. 가, 없어요   5. 이, 있어요

Practice Activity 6
1. 남동생이 없어요   2. 친구가 있어요   3. 시간이 없어요   4. 가방이 있어요
5. 신발이 없어요

Practice Activity 7
1. 엄마   → c. 어머니, f. 어머님
2. 아빠   → a. 아버지, e. 아버님
3. 부모   → d. 부모님
4. 할머니 → b. 할머님

Practice Activity 8
1. 그럴게요   → b. I will do it in that way.
2. 거실   → e. living room/family room
3. 인사 드리다 → f. to greet (honorific form)
4. 부모   → c. parents
5. 계시다   → d. to exist (honorific form)
6. 할머니   → a. grandmother

Practice Activity 9
1. 할머님   2. 부장님   3. 이 교수님   4. 팀장님   5. 남동생

LESSON 6
Practice Activity 1
1. 에   → d. at, to
2. 에서   → a. at, from B
3. 고객   → b. a customer
4. 빠르다 → e. to be quick
5. 어떻게 → c. how
6. 까지   → f. up to a certain point

Practice Activity 2
1. 에서   2. 에   3. 에서   4. 에서   5. 에

Practice Activity 3
1. 에서, 까지   2. 에서   3. 에   4. 까지   5. 으로   6. 으로

Practice Activity 4
1. 다음달   2. 교통   3. 수단   4. 이용하다   5. 버스   6. 택시

Practice Activity 5
1. 을   2. 를   3. 를   4. 을   5. 를

Practice Activity 6
1. 차를   2. 택시를   3. 버스 정류장이   4. 지하철이   5. 기차를, 기차역이

Practice Activity 7
1. 공원   → park
2. 거기   → there
3. 여기   → here
4. 역사   → history
5. 내리다   → get off
6. 시장   → market
7. 문화   → culture
8. 되다/돼다   → be done, become

Practice Activity 8
1. 나 영국사람이다   2. 민수 여행하고 있어요   3. 사라 학교 가고 있어요
4. 철수 한국 갔어요

Practice Activity 9
1. 만삼천칠백원   2. 사만팔천원   3. 오만이천육십원   4. 팔십구만칠백원
5. 칠십억

LESSON 7
Practice Activity 1
1. Straight (direction) → d. 직진
2. Payment   → c. 계산
3. Cash   → e. 현금
4. Direction   → f. 쪽
5. Empty car, vacant → a. 빈차
6. Driver   → b. 기사

Practice Activity 2
1. 오른쪽으로 가 주세요.   2. 왼쪽으로 가 주세요.   3. 지하철로 가 주세요
4. 경복궁으로 가 주세요.   5. 홍대역으로 가 주세요.

Practice Activity 3
1. 서울역으로 가 주세요.   2. 공항으로 가 주세요.   3. 시장으로 가 주세요.
4. 서울대로 가 주세요.   5. 롯데월드로 가 주세요.

Practice Activity 4
1. time → 번   2. bottles → 병   3. paper → 장   4. cars → 대
5. books → 권   6. people → 명   7. items → 개   8. animals → 마리
9. buildings → 채 10. glasses → 잔

Practice Activity 5

1. How many people?   → f. 몇 명이에요?
2. How many animals?   → c. 몇 마리예요?
3. How many bottles?   → d. 몇 병이에요?
4. How many pieces of paper? → a. 몇 장이에요?
5. How many times did you go? → e. 몇 번 갔어요?
6. How many books?   → b. 몇 권이에요?

Practice Activity 6

1. 다섯 마리예요.   2. 세 대예요.   3. 열 두 명이에요.   4. 여덟 번 갔어요.
5. 두 개예요.   6. 한 장이에요.   7. 일곱 병이에요.

Practice Activity 7

1. 편도   2. 시간표   3. Round-trip   4. -행   5. To arrive   6. 요금
7. To purchase

Practice Activity 8

1. 에   2. 에   3. 에서   4. 에서   5. 에

Practice Activity 9

1. 에서   2. 에   3. 에서   4. 에서   5. 에

Practice Activity 10

a) 안녕하세요.   b) 행   c) 기차   d) 도착   e) 왕복은   f) 기차   g) 부산

LESSON 8
Practice Activity 1

1. 제일   2. 좋아하다   3. 래퍼   4. 가수   5. 공연   6. 음악

Practice Activity 2

1. Akira 씨, 일본 사람이에요, 중국 사람이에요?
2. John 씨, 야구 좋아해요, 농구 좋아해요?
3. 의건 씨, 강아지 키워요, 고양이 키워요?
4. 지수 씨, 노래방에 갈까요, 영화 보러 갈까요?

Practice Activity 3

1. 버스 탈래요, 기차 탈래요?
2. 파스타 좋아해요, 피자 좋아해요?
3. 불고기 좋아해요, 떡볶이 좋아해요?
4. 1학년이에요, 2학년이에요?

Practice Activity 4

1. old   → e. 오래되다   4. worldwide/global → f. 세계적
2. famous   → d. 유명하다   5. historical drama → c. 사극
3. act/performance → b. 연기   6. actor   → a. 배우

Practice Activity 5
1. 안   2. 안   3. 못   4. 안

Practice Activity 6
1. 아니요, 일본 음식을 많이 안 먹어요.
2. 아니요, 그 여배우는 안 예뻐요.
3. 아니요, 케이팝 (K-Pop)을 많이 안 들어요.

Practice Activity 7
1. 아니요, 주말에 서울에 못 놀러 가요.
2. 아니요, 오늘 수업에 못 가요.
3. 아니요, 매운 음식 잘 못 먹어요.
4. 아니요, 어제 숙제를 다 못 했어요.

Practice Activity 8
1. 롯데 월드   →   c. lotte World
2. 입장료   →   g. admission
3. 비싸다   →   f. expensive
4. 놀이 공원   →   e. amusement Park
5. 놀이 기구   →   d. ride (at an amusement park)
6. 먹을거리   →   a. food
7. 쉬다   →   b. to rest

Practice Activity 9
1. 한국의 문화   2. 제이크의 전공   3. 남동생의 신발   4. 민지의 형제자매
5. 지수의 친구

Practice Activity 10
1. 수지는 저의 룸메이트 입니다.
2. 그것은 잭의 카드입니다. / 그 카드는 잭의 것입니다.
3. 제이크는 저의 남동생입니다.
4. 그것은 민지의 컴퓨터입니다. / 그 컴퓨터는 민지의 것입니다.
5. 그것은 민영이의 텔레비전입니다. / 그 텔레비전은 민영이의 것입니다.

LESSON 9
Practice Activity 1
1. 로   2. 로   3. 로   4. 로   5. 로

Practice Activity 2
1. 로   2. 으로   3. 으로   4. 으로   5. 으로

Practice Activity 3
1. Place   2. The equipment to complete an action   3. Transportation   4. Place
5. The equipment to complete an action

Practice Activity 4
1. Irregular   2. Regular   3. Irregular   4. Regular   5. Irregular

Practice Activity 5
1. 도와요   2. 도왔어요   3. 돕겠어요   4. 도운   5. 도울

Practice Activity 7
1. The teacher's book   →   e. 선생님의 책
2. My girlfriend   →   d. 내 여자친구
3. My house   →   a. 내 집
4. Mother's food   →   c. 어머니의 음식
5. My friend's restaurant →   b. 내 친구의 음식점

Practice Activity 9
1. 제 나라의 문화는 달라요.
2. 책의 어머니는 선생님입니다.
3. 네 차 멋있다.
4. 제 친구의 집은 한국에 있습니다.

LESSON 10
Practice Activity 1
1. 보아요/보어요
2. 해어요/해요
3. 내랴요/내려요
4. 드샤요/드셔요
5. 예빠요/예뻐요

Practice Activity 2
1. 나가요   2. 꿈꿔요   3. 도와줘요   4. 물어봐요   5. 벗어요
6. 사요   7. 서둘러요   8. 소개해요   9. 와요   10. 이겨요
11. 재요   12. 줘요   13. 져요   14. 해요   15. 타요

Practice Activity 3
1. 아프다   2. 꿈꿔요   3. 피곤하다   4. 보다   5. 공부하다

Practice Activity 5
1. 먹었다   2. 췄다   3. 만들었다   4. 앉았다   5. 일어났다
6. 공부했다   3. 기다렸다   8. 대화했다   9. 살았다   10. 보냈다
11. 기억했다   12. 도착했다 13. 끝났다   14. 약속했다

Practice Activity 6
1. 나는 어제 서울에 도착했다.   4. 나는 이 씨에게 내 숙제를 줬다.
2. 세종대왕은 600년 전에 살았다.   5. 김치를 먹었어?
3. 우리는 어제 대화를 했었다.   6. 어제 편지를 보냈어?

Practice Activity 7

1. Correct   2. Correct   3. Correct   4. Correct   5. Correct

LESSON 11

Practice Activity 1

1. 안 드세요? /
   드시지 않으세요?
2. 안 드세요? / 드시지 않으세요?
3. 결혼하지 않으세요?
4. 안 주무세요? /
   주무시지 않으세요?
5. 안 주무세요? /
   주무시지 않으세요?
6. 사용하지 않으세요?

Practice Activity 2

1. 네   2. 네   2. 아니요   3. 아니요   4. 네   5. 네

Practice Activity 3

Words	Present tense	Present tense - question	Past tense	Future tense (will)
공부하다	공부합니다.	공부합니까?	공부했습니다.	공부하겠습니다.
듣다	듣습니다.	듣습니까?	들었습니다.	듣겠습니다.
생각하다	생각합니다.	생각합니까?	생각했습니다.	생각하겠습니다.
연락하다	연락합니다.	연락합니까?	연락했습니다.	연락하겠습니다.
두다	둡니다.	둡니까?	두었습니다.	두겠습니다.

Practice Activity 4

1. 당신은 한국에 사십니까?
2. 저는 미국에 삽니다.
3. 저는 내일 학교에 가겠습니다.
4. 저는 오후에 음악을 듣겠습니다.
5. 저는 매일 숙제를 합니다.
6. 저는 어머니를 돕겠습니다.
7. 시험은 어려웠습니다.

Practice Activity 5

1. 있습니다.   2. 청소를 끝냈습니다.   3. 입니다.   4. 알겠습니다.

Practice Activity 6

1. 그렇게   2. 얼만큼   3. 어떻게   4. 이런   5. 저

Practice Activity 8

	이것	저것	그것	어느 것
Far from both speaker and listener		x		
Far from speaker and close to listener			x	
Close to speaker and far from listener	x			
Close to both speaker and listener	x			
Abstract object			x	x
Which				x

Korean-English Dictionary

-개 **gae** counter (number of items)
-번 **beon** a number (line no.1, line no. 2, etc.)
-행 **haeng** train destination
(신용)카드 **(sinyong) kadeu** credit card
-습니다 **sumnida** high form verb ending
-이다 **ida** be (to be)
-지 않다 **ji anta** not be (to not be) (preceded by a verb)
K-pop Korean pop music

ㄱ

가격 **gagyeok** price
가깝다 **gakkapda** close (to)
가끔 **gakkeum** sometimes
가방 **gabang** bag
가볍다 **gabyeopda** light
가수 **gasu** singer
가을 **gaeul** fall
갈비 **galbi** *Galbi*
갈아타다 **garatada** transfer
감사하다 **gamsahada** thankful
감천문화마을 **gamcheonmunhwamaeul** Gamcheon Culture Village
강의실 **ganguisil** classroom
같이 **gachi** together
거기 (그) **geogi(geu)** that (close to listener)
거스름돈 **geoseureumdon** change
거울 **geoul** mirror
걱정하다 **geokjeonghada** worry
건강 **geongang** health
겨울 **gyeoul** winter
결제 **gyeolje** payment
결혼 **gyeolhon** marriage
결혼하다 **gyeolhonhada** to marry (to get married)
경복궁 **gyeongbokgung** Gyeongbokgung Palace
계산 **gyesan** payment
계절 **gyejeol** season
고객님 **gogaengnim** customer
고기집 **gogitjip** restaurant specializing in meat
고향 **gohyang** hometown
공부하다 **gongbuhada** study
공연 **gongyeon** concert, performance
공원 **gongwon** park
공항 **gonghang** airport
공항철도 **gonghangcheoldo** airport railroad
과자 **gwaja** snack
관습 **gwanseup** custom

광안대교 **gwangandaegyo** Gwangan Bridge
광주 **gwangju** Gwangju
광화문광장 **gwanghwamungwangjang** Gwanghwamun Plaza
괜찮다 **gwaenchanta** okay/fine (to be okay/to be fine)
교통 **gyotong** transportation
교통카드 **gyotongkadeu** transportation card
구경 **gugyeong** sightseeing
구경하다 **gugyeonghada** sightsee
구매하다 **gumaehada** purchase
국기 **gukgi** national flag
국립민속박물관 **gungnimminsokbangmulgwan** National Folk Museum of Korea
국립중앙박물관 **gungnipjungangbangmulgwan** National Museum of Korea
귀 **gwi** ear
귀엽다 **gwiyeopda** cute (to be cute)
그래서 **geuraeseo** so
그러면 **geureomyeon** if so
그렇군요 **geureokunyo** I see
근처 **geuncheo** vicinity
금요일 **geumyoil** Friday
기념품 **ginyeompum** souvenir
기말 **gimal** final
기쁘다 **gippeuda** happy (to be happy)
기사님 **gisanim** driver
기차 **gicha** train
기차역 **gichayeok** train station
기차표 **gichapyo** train ticket
김밥 **gimbap** *Gimbap*
김치찌개 **gimchijjigae** *Kimchijjigae*, a spicy stew made of kimchi, onion, tofu, meat and kimchi juice
김포국제공항 **gimpogukjegonghang** Gimpo International Airport
김해국제공항 **gimhaegukjegonghang** Gimhae International Airport
까지 **kkaji** up to a certain point
끝나다 **kkeunnada** end

ㄴ

나라 **nara** country
나중 **najung** later
난방 **nanbang** heating
날씨 **nalssi** weather
남기다 **namgida** leave behind
남다 **namda** remain
남대문시장 **namdaemunsijang**

Namdaemun Market
남동생 **namdongsaeng** younger brother
남산 **namsan** Namsan Mountain
낫다 **natda** better (to be better)
낮잠 **natjam** nap
내리다 **naerida** get off/out (to get off/to get out)
내일 **naeil** tomorrow
냉면 **naengmyeon** Naengmyeon
냉장고 **naengjanggo** refrigerator
네이버 **neibeo** NAVER (portal site)
넷플릭스 **netpeullikseu** Netflix
노트 **noteu** notebook
노트북 **noteubuk** laptop
놀이 공원 **nori gongwon** amusement park
놀이 기구 **nori gigu** ride (amusement park)
누나 **nuna** older sister of a male
눈 **nun** eye
뉴질랜드 **nyujillaendeu** New Zealand
늦다 **neutda** late (to be late)
님 **nim** honorific suffix

ㄷ

다니다 **danida** commute, go to and from, attend
다시 **dasi** again
다음달 **daeumdal** next month
단추 **danchu** button
달 **dal** month
당연하다 **dangyeonhada** natural (to be natural), of course
대구 **daegu** Daegu
대전 **daejeon** Daejeon
대하다 **daehada** about, regard
덕분에 **deokbune** thanks to
덕수궁 **deoksugung** Deoksugung Palace
덥다 **deopda** hot (to be hot)
데 **de** place
도착하다 **dochakada** arrive
독일 **dogil** Germany
돕다 **dopda** help
동대문디자인플라자 **dongdaemundijain-peullaja** Dongdaemun Design Plaza
동생 **dongsaeng** younger sibling
동전 **dongjeon** coin
되다/돼다 **doeda/dwaeda** be done, become
  (됐다 **doetda** = 되었다 **doeeotda**)
된장찌개 **doenjangjjigae** *doenjangjjiage* bean paste stew
두다 **duda** leave, put
둘 다 **dul da** both
드라마 **deurama** drama
드라이기 **deuraigi** hair dryer
드시다 **deusida** eat (honorific)
듣다 **deutda** hear, listen, take a class
들어가다 **deureogada** go in
들어오다 **deureooda** come in
따뜻하다 **ttatteutada** warm (to be warm)

때 **ttae** time
떡 **tteok** rice cake
또 **tto** again, also

ㄹ

라면 **ramyeon** instant noodles
래퍼 **raepeo** rapper rap artist
러시아 **reosia** Russia
롤러코스터 **rolleokoseuteo** roller coaster
롯데 월드 **rotde woldeu** Lotte World
롯데월드타워 **rotdewoldeutawo** Lotte World Tower
룸메이트 **rummeiteu** roommate
리조트 **rijoteu** resort
린스 **rinseu** rinse

ㅁ

마다 **mada** every, each
마트 **mateu** mart
만나다 **mannada** meet
만두 **mandu** dumpling
만원 **manwon** 10,000 won
맑다 **makda** sunny (weather), clear
맛집 **matjip** must-eat place
맞다 **matda** correct (to be correct), right (to be right) (agreeing with another's opinion)
매일 **maeil** everyday
매표소 **maepyoso** ticket office
맵다 **maepda** spicy (to be spicy)
머그잔 **meogeujan** mug
머리 **meori** head
먹다 **meokda** eat
먹을거리 **meogeulgeori** food
멀다 **meolda** far (to be far)
멕시코 **meksiko** Mexico
면세점 **myeonsejeom** duty free shop
명 **myeong** general counting word for people
명동 **myeongdong** Myeong-dong
몇 **myeot** how many/a few
모두 **modu** all
모르다 **moreuda** not know
목 **mok** neck
목요일 **mogyoil** Thursday
몸 **mom** body
무겁다 **mugeopda** heavy (to be heavy)
문 **mun** door
문화 **munhwa** culture
문화상품권 **munhwasangpumgwon** gift voucher
뭐 **mwo** what
미국 **miguk** America
미국인 **migugin** American
미역국 **miyeokguk** seaweed soup
밀면 **milmyeon** wheat noodles

ㅂ

바다 **bada** ocean
바닥 **badak** floor
바디워시 **badiwosi** body wash
바로 **baro** directly/straight
바쁘다 **bappeuda** busy (to be busy)
반갑다 **bangapda** nice to meet (to be nice to meet)
발 **bal** foot
밤 **bam** night
밥 **bap** rice, food
방 **bang** room
방문하다 **bangmunhada** visit
방향 **banghyang** direction
배 **bae** abdomen, boat, ship
배고프다 **baegopeuda** hungry (to be hungry)
배우 **baeu** actor
배우다 **baeuda** learn
백원 **baegwon** 100 won
백화점 **baekwajeom** department store
버스 **beoseu** bus
벗다 **beotda** take off
별로 **byeollo** particular (별로이다 **byelloida** = not particularly fond of it), not very
병원 **byeongwon** hospital
보다 **boda** see/watch
보여주다 **boyeojuda** show
볼펜 **bolpen** ballpoint pen
봄 **bom** spring
뵈다 **boeda** high form for the word "to meet"
부르다 **bureuda** call
부산 **busan** Busan
북촌한옥마을 **bukchonhanongmaeul** Bukchon Hanok Village
분 **bun** honorific counting word for people
뷔페 **bwipe** buffet
비빔밥 **bibimbap** *Bibimbap*
비싸다 **bissada** expensive
비자 **bija** visa
비행기 **bihaenggi** airplane
빈차 **bincha** empty car, vacant
빠르다 **ppareuda** quick (to be quick), fast
빵 **ppang** bread

ㅅ

사극 **sageuk** historical drama
사다 **sada** buy
사용하다 **sayonghada** use
산책 **sanchaek** walk
산책하다 **sanchaekada** take a walk
삼겹살 **samgyeopsal** pork belly
새벽 **saebyeok** early morning/dawn
샌드위치 **saendeuwichi** sandwich
생각하다 **seanggakada** think
생물학 **saengmulhak** biology

샴푸 **syampu** shampoo
서양 **seoyang** the West
서울 **seoul** Seoul
서울역 **seoul-yeok** Seoul Station
선배 **seonbae** senior
선풍기 **seonpunggi** electric fan
세계적 **segyejeok** worldwide/global
세탁기 **setakgi** washing machine
세탁하다 **setakada** do the laundry
소파 **sopa** sofa, couch
손 **son** hand
손가락 **songarak** finger
수단 **sudan** means, method
수업 **sueop** class
수업을 듣다 **sueobeul deutda** take a class
수영장 **suyeongjang** swimming pool
수요일 **suyoil** Wednesday
수하물 **suhamul** luggage
순두부찌개 **sundubujjigae** soft tofu stew
숟가락 **sutgarak** spoon
쉬다 **swida** rest
쉽다 **swipda** easy
스웨덴 **seuweden** Sweden
스트리밍 서비스 **seuteuriming seobiseu** streaming service
스페인 **seupein** Spain
승강장 **seunggangjang** station platform
시간 **sigan** time
시간표 **siganpyo** time table
시계 **sigye** clock
시장 **sijang** market
시차 **sicha** time difference
시키다 **sikida** cause something (to cause something), order food
시험 **siheom** exam
식기세척기 **sikgisecheokgi** dishwasher
식사(하다) **siksa(hada)** meal (to have a meal)
식탁 **siktak** dining table
신발 **sinbal** shoes
신발장 **sinbaljang** shoe closet
신호등 **sinhodeung** traffic lights
싫어하다 **sireohada** dislike (to dislike)
싸다 **ssada** cheap (to be cheap)
쓰다 **sseuda** use

ㅇ

아니다 **anida** you're welcome (basic meaning is "no.")
아이스크림 **aiseukeurim** ice cream
아침 **achim** breakfast, morning
아케이드 **akeideu** arcade
아프다 **apeuda** hurt (to be hurt), sick (to be sick)
아프리카 **apeurika** Africa
안되다 **andoeda** not be okay (to not be okay)
않다 **anta** not be (to not be)
알겠다 **algetda** I see

알다 **alda** know
액자 **aekja** frame
야구장 **yagujang** baseball stadium
약국 **yakguk** pharmacy
약속 **yaksok** appointment/promise
어깨 **eokkae** shoulder
어느 **eoneu** which
어디 **eodi** where
어때 **eottae** how
어떻게 **eotteoke** how
어렵다 **eoryeopda** hard to do
어서오세요 **eoseooseyo** welcome
어제 **eoje** yesterday
얼굴 **eolgul** face
얼마 **eolma** how much
없다 **eopda** not exist
에버랜드 **ebeoraendeu** Everland
에어컨 **eeokeon** air conditioner
여권 **yeogwon** passport
여기(이) **yeogi(i)** this (close to speaker)
여동생 **yeodongsaeng** younger sister
여름 **yeoreum** summer
여분 **yeobun** extra
여행 **yeohaeng** travel
역 **yeok** subway station
역사 **yeoksa** history
연기 **yeongi** act, performance
연락하다 **yeollakada** contact
연필 **yeonpil** pencil
열쇠고리 **yeolsoegori** key chain
엽서 **yeopseo** postcard
영국 **yeongguk** the United Kingdom
영수증 **yeongsujeung** receipt
영어 **yeongeo** English
영화 **yeonghwa** movie
영화관 **yeonghwagwan** movie theater
옆 **yeop** next to
예 **ye** manners
예쁘다 **yeppeuda** pretty (to be pretty)
예술의 전당 **yesuruijeondang** Seoul Arts Center
예약 **yeyak** reservation, booking
예의 **yeui** etiquette, formalities, manners
오늘 **oneul** today
오다 **oda** come (to come)
오래되다 **oraedoeda** old
오랜만이다 **oraenmanida** long time (long time no see)
오른 **oreun** right (direction)
오만원 **omanwon** 50,000 won
오천원 **ocheonwon** 5,000 won
오후 **ohu** afternoon
온돌 **ondol** under-floor heating system
옷장 **otjang** closet
와 **wa** wow
왕복 **wangbok** round trip
외식 **oesik** eating outside

왼 **oen** left (direction)
요금 **yogeum** fare
우산 **usan** umbrella
우와 **uwa** wow
우체국 **ucheguk** post office
운동 **undong** exercise
울산 **ulsan** Ulsan
월요일 **woryoil** Monday
유명하다 **yumyeonghada** famous
유심칩 **yusimchip** Sim card
유학생 **yuhaksaeng** international student
은행 **eunhaeng** bank
음료 **eumnyo** drink
음악 **eumak** music
의자 **uija** chair
이따 **itta** later
이름 **ireum** name
이메일 **imeil** email
이용하다 **iyonghada** use, utilize
이탈리아 **itallia** Italy
이태리 **itaeri** Italian
인분 **inbun** counter for number of servings (ex: 4 인분 means a dish prepared for 4 people)
인스타그램 **inseutageuraem** Instagram
인천 **Incheon** Incheon
인천국제공항 **incheongukjegonghang** Incheon International Airport
인형 **inhyeong** doll
일 **il** work
일본 **ilbon** Japan
일본인 **ilbonin** Japanese
일요일 **iryoil** Sunday
일주일 **iljuil** a week
읽다 **ikda** read
입 **ip** mouth
입구 **ipgu** (subway station) entrance
입장료 **ipjangnyo** admission

ㅈ

자다 **jada** sleep
자동차 **jadongcha** car
자석 **jaseok** magnet
장마 **jangma** rainy season
장식품 **jangsikpum** ornament
재미있다 **jaemiitda** fun/interesting (to be fun/to be interesting)
저기(저) **jeogi(jeo)** that (not close to either the listener or speaker)
저녁 **jeonyeok** dinner, evening
전공 **jeongong** major
전기밥솥 **jeongibapsot** electric rice cooker
전망대 **jeonmangdae** observatory
전시회 **jeonsihoe** exhibition
전자레인지 **jeonjareinji** microwave (oven)
전주 한옥마을 **jeonjuhanongmaeul** Jeonju Hanok Village

전철 **jeoncheol** subway
전화 **jeonhwa** call
전화번호 **jeonhwabeonho** phone number
점심 **jeomsim** lunch, noon
접시 **jeopsi** dish
젓가락 **jeotgarak** chopsticks
정거장 **jeonggeojang** subway stop
정류장 **jeongnyujang** station
정리하다 **jeongnihada** organize (to organize)
제일 **jeil** most, first
조식 **josik** breakfast
조심하다 **josimhada** careful (to be careful)
존경 **jongyeong** respect
좀 **jom** (short for 조금 **jogeum**) bit, little
좋다 **jota** good (to be good)
좋아하다 **joahada** favorite, like
좌석번호 **jwaseokbeonho** the seat number
주다 **juda** give
주말 **jumal** weekend
주먹밥 **jumeokbap** rice balls
주무시다 **jumusida** sleep (honorific)
주문하다 **jumunhada** order food
주스 **juseu** juice
주차 **jucha** parking
주차장 **juchajang** parking lot
중국 **jungguk** China
중국인 **junggugin** Chinese
중요하다 **jungyohada** important
지금 **jigeum** now
지내다 **jinaeda** spend (time)
지폐 **jipye** bill, paper money
지하철 **jihacheol** subway (underground)
지하층 **jihacheung** underground/basement
직진 **jikjin** straight (direction)
진짜 **jinjja** really
집 **jip** home
쪽 **jjok** direction
찜질방 **jjiljilbang** Korean dry sauna

ㅊ

창경궁 **changgyeonggung** Changgyeonggung
  Palace
창덕궁 **changdeokgung** Changdeokgung
  Palace
창문 **changmun** window
책 **chaek** book
책상 **chaeksang** desk
책장 **chaekjang** bookshelf
처음 **cheoeum** first
천원 **cheonwon** 1,000 won
청계천 **cheonggyecheon** Cheonggyecheon
  Stream
청소하다 **cheongsohada** clean
청와대 **cheongwadae** the Blue House
초대하다 **chodaehada** invite
최고 **choego** the best

출구 **chulgu** (subway station) exit
춥다 **chupda** cold (to be cold)
충전기 **chungjeongi** charger
치약 **chiyak** toothpaste
친구 **chingu** friend
침대 **chimdae** bed
칫솔 **chitsol** toothbrush
카카오톡 **kakaotok** Kakaotalk (SNS)
카페 **kape** café
캐나다 **kaenada** Canada
커피 **keopi** coffee
컴퓨터 **keompyuteo** computer
코 **ko** nose
콘서트 **konseoteu** concert

ㅌ

타다 **tada** ride (a car, train, or bike)
탑승권 **tapseunggwon** boarding pass
택배 **taekbae** package
택시 **taeksi** taxi
텔레비전 **tellebijeon** television
토요일 **toyoil** Saturday
티켓 **tiket** ticket

ㅍ

파스타 **paseuta** pasta
파티 **pati** party
팔찌 **paljji** bracelet
페이스북 **peiseubuk** Facebook
편도 **pyeondo** one-way trip
표현 **pyohyeon** expression
푸드코트 **pudeukoteu** food court
프랑스 **peurangseu** France
피곤하다 **pigonhada** tired (to be tired)
피자 **pija** pizza
필요없다 **piryoeopda** no need

ㅎ

하다 **hada** do
학교 **hakgyo** school
한강 **hangang** Han River
한국 **hanguk** South Korea
한국인 **hangugin** Korean
한라산 **hallasan** Hallasan Mountain
한복 **hanbok** Korean traditional clothes
한식 **hansik** Korean food
할인 **harin** discount
해동용궁사 **haedongyonggungsa** Haedong
  Yonggungsa Temple
해운대 **haeundae** Haeundae
핸드폰 **haendeupon** cellphone
햄버거 **haembeogeo** hamburger
행복하다 **haengbokada** happy (to be happy)
향수 **hyangsu** perfume
현관 **hyeongwan** porch
현금 **hyeongeum** cash

형 **hyeong** older brother of a male
형제 **hyeongje** siblings
호선 **hoseon** subway line, line
호주 **hoju** Australia
호텔 **hotel** hotel
혹시 **hoksi** perchance, maybe
화요일 **hwayoil** Tuesday

화장실 **hwajangsil** restroom
환승하다 **hwanseunghada** transfer
회사 **hoesa** company
휴가 **hyuga** break, vacation
흐리다 **heurida** cloudy
힘들다 **himdeulda** straining/exhausting (to be straining / to be exhausting)

English–Korean Dictionary

1,000 won **cheonwon** 천원
10,000 won **manwon** 만원
100 won **baegwon** 백원
5,000 won **ocheonwon** 오천원
50,000 won **omanwon** 오만원

A

a few **myeot** 몇
a number (gate no.1, gate no. 2, etc.) **beon** -번
a week **iljuil** 일주일
abdomen **bae** 배
about **daehada** 대하다
act **yeongi** 연기
actor **baeu** 배우
admission **ipjangnyo** 입장료
Africa **apeurika** 아프리카
afternoon **ohu** 오후
again **dasi** 다시
again **tto** 또
air conditioner **eeokeon** 에어컨
airplane **bihaenggi** 비행기
airport **gonghang** 공항
airport railroad **gonghangcheoldo** 공항철도
all **modu** 모두
also **tto** 또
America **miguk** 미국
American **migugin** 미국인
amusement park **nori gongwon** 놀이 공원
appointment **yaksok** 약속
arcade **akeideu** 아케이드
arrive **dochak** 도착
attend **danida** 다니다
Australia **hoju** 호주

B

bag **gabang** 가방
ballpoint pen **bolpen** 볼펜
bank **eunhaeng** 은행
baseball stadium **yagujang** 야구장

basement **jihacheung** 지하층
be (to be) **ida** ~이다
bean paste stew **doenjangjjiage** 된장찌개
become **doeda/dwaeda** 되다/돼다
bed **chimdae** 침대
better (to be better) **natda** 낫다
Bibimbap **bibimbap** 비빔밥
bill **jipye** 지폐
biology **saengmulhak** 생물학
bit **jom** 좀 (short form for 조금 **jogeum**)
boarding pass **tapseunggwon** 탑승권
boat **bae** 배
body **mom** 몸
body wash **badiwosi** 바디워시
book **chaek** 책
booking **yeyak** 예약
bookshelf **chaekjang** 책장
both **dul da** 둘 다
bracelet **paljji** 팔찌
bread **ppang** 빵
break **hyuga** 휴가
breakfast **josik** 조식
breakfast **achim** 아침
buffet **bwipe** 뷔페
Bukchon Hanok Village **bukchonhanong-maeul** 북촌한옥마을
bus **beoseu** 버스
Busan **busan** 부산
busy (to be busy) **bappeuda** 바쁘다
button **danchu** 단추
buy **sada** 사다

C

café **kape** 카페
call **bureuda** 부르다
call **jeonhwa** 전화
Canada **kaenada** 캐나다
car **jadongcha** 자동차
careful (to be careful) **josimhada** 조심하다

cash **hyeongeum** 현금
cause something (to cause something) **sikida** 시키다
cellphone **haendeupon** 핸드폰
chair **uija** 의자
Changdeokgung Palace **changdeokgung** 창덕궁
change **geoseureumdon** 거스름돈
Changgyeonggung Palace **changgyeonggung** 창경궁
charger **chungjeongi** 충전기
cheap (to be cheap) **ssada** 싸다
Cheonggyecheon Stream **cheonggyecheon** 청계천
China **jungguk** 중국
Chinese **junggugin** 중국인
chopsticks **jeotgarak** 젓가락
class **sueop** 수업
classroom **ganguisil** 강의실
clean **cheongsohada** 청소하다
clock **sigye** 시계
close (to) **gakkapda** 가깝다
closet **otjang** 옷장
cloudy **heurida** 흐리다
coffee **keopi** 커피
coin **dongjeon** 동전
cold (to be cold) **chupda** 춥다
come in **deureooda** 들어오다
come **oda** 오다
come to **oda** 오다
commute **danida** 다니다
company **hoesa** 회사
computer **keompyuteo** 컴퓨터
concert **gongyeon** 공연
concert **konseoteu** 콘서트
contact **yeollakada** 연락하다
correct (to be correct) (agreeing to other's opinion) **matda** 맞다
cosmetic products **hwajangpum** 화장품
couch **sopa** 소파
counter (number of items) **gae** 개
counter for number of servings **inbun** 인분
country **nara** 나라
credit card **(sinyong) kadeu** (신용)카드
culture **munhwa** 문화
custom **gwanseup** 관습
customer **gogaengnim** 고객님 (님 **nim** is an honorific suffix)
cute (to be cute) **gwiyeopda** 귀엽다

D

Daegu **daegu** 대구
Daejeon **daejeon** 대전
dawn **saebyeok** 새벽
Deoksugung Palace **deoksugung** 덕수궁
department store **baekwajeom** 백화점

desk **chaeksang** 책상
dining table **siktak** 식탁
dinner **jeonyeok** 저녁
direction **banghyang** 방향
direction **jjok** 쪽
directly **baro** 바로
discount **harin** 할인
dish **jeopsi** 접시
dishwasher **sikgisecheokgi** 식기세척기
dislike (to dislike) **sireohada** 싫어하다
do **hada** 하다
do the laundry **setakada** 세탁하다
doll **inhyeong** 인형
Dongdaemun Design Plaza **dongdaemundijainpeullaja** 동대문디자인플라자
door **mun** 문
drama **deurama** 드라마
drink **eumnyo** 음료
driver **gisanim** 기사님
dumpling **mandu** 만두
duty free shop **myeonsejeom** 면세점

E

each **mada** 마다
Ear **gwi** 귀
early morning **saebyeok** 새벽
easy **swipda** 쉽다
eat (honorific) **deusida** 드시다
eat **meokda** 먹다
eating outside **oesik** 외식
electric fan **seonpunggi** 선풍기
electric rice cooker **jeongibapsot** 전기밥솥
email **imeil** 이메일
empty car **bin cha** 빈 차
end **kkeunnada** 끝나다
English **yeongeo** 영어
entrance (subway station) **ipgu** 입구
etiquette **yeui** 예의
Everland **ebeoraendeu** 에버랜드
every **mada** 마다
everyday **maeil** 매일
exam **siheom** 시험
exercise **undong** 운동
exhausting (to be exhausting) **himdeulda** 힘들다
exhibition **jeonsihoe** 전시회
exit (subway station) **chulgu** 출구
expensive **bissada** 비싸다
expression **pyohyeon** 표현
extra **yeobun** 여분
eye **nun** 눈

F

face **eolgul** 얼굴
Facebook **peiseubuk** 페이스북

fall **gaeul** 가을
famous **yumyeonghada** 유명하다
far (to be far) **meolda** 멀다
fare **yogeum** 요금
fast **ppareuda** 빠르다
favorite **joahada** 좋아하다
final **gimal** 기말
fine (to be fine) **gwaenchanta** 괜찮다
finger **songarak** 손가락
first **cheoeum** 처음
first **jeil** 제일
floor **badak** 바닥
food **bap** 밥
food court **pudeukoteu** 푸드코트
food **meogeulgeori** 먹을거리
foot **bal** 발
formalities **yeui** 예의
frame **aekja** 액자
France **peurangseu** 프랑스
Friday **geumyoil** 금요일
friend **chingu** 친구
fun (to be fun) **jaemiitda** 재미있다

G
Galbi **galbi** 갈비
Gamcheon Culture Village
  gamcheonmunhwamaeul 감천문화마을
Germany **dogil** 독일
get off **naerida** 내리다
get out **naerida** 내리다
gift voucher **munhwasangpumgwon**
  문화상품권
Gimbap **gimbap** 김밥
Gimhae International Airport
  gimhaegukjegonghang 김해국제공항
Gimpo International Airport
  gimpogukjegonghang 김포국제공항
give **juda** 주다
global **segyejeok** 세계적
go in **deureogada** 들어가다
go to and from **danida** 다니다
good (to be good) **jota** 좋다
Gwangan Bridge **gwangandaegyo** 광안대교
Gwanghwamun Plaza
  gwanghwamungwangjang 광화문광장
Gwangju **gwangju** 광주
Gyeongbokgung Palace **gyeongbokgung**
  경복궁

H
Haedong Yonggungsa Temple
  haedongyonggungsa 해동용궁사
Haeundae **haeundae** 해운대
hair dryer **deuraigi** 드라이기
Hallasan Mountain **hallasan** 한라산
hamburger **haembeogeo** 햄버거

Han River **hangang** 한강
hand **son** 손
happy (to be happy) **gippeuda** 기쁘다
happy (to be happy) **haengbokada** 행복하다
hard to do **eoryeopda** 어렵다
have a meal (to have a meal) **siksahada**
  식사하다
head **meori** 머리
health **geongang** 건강
hear **deutda** 듣다
heating **nanbang** 난방
heavy (to be heavy) **mugeopda** 무겁다
help **dopda** 돕다
high form for the word "to meet" **boeda** 뵈다
high form verb ending **seumnida** ~습니다
historical drama **sageuk** 사극
history **yeoksa** 역사
home **jip** 집
hometown **gohyang** 고향
honorific counting word for people **bun** 분
honorific suffix **nim** 님
hospital **byeongwon** 병원
hot (to be hot) **deopda** 덥다
hotel **hotel** 호텔
how **eottae** 어때
how **eotteoke** 어떻게
how many **myeot** 몇
how much **eolma** 얼마
hungry (to be hungry) **baegopeuda** 배고프다
hurt (to be hurt) **apeuda** 아프다

I
I see **algetda** 알겠다
I see **geureokunyo** 그렇군요
ice cream **aiseukeurim** 아이스크림
if so **geureomyeon** 그러면
important **jungyohada** 중요하다
Incheon **incheon** 인천
Incheon International Airport
  incheongukjegonghang 인천국제공항
Instagram **inseutageuraem** 인스타그램
instant noodles **ramyeon** 라면
interesting (to be interesting) **jaemiitda**
  재미있다
international student **yuhaksaeng** 유학생
invite **chodaehada** 초대하다
Italian **itaeri** 이태리
Italy **itallia** 이탈리아

J
Japan **ilbon** 일본
Japanese **ilbonin** 일본인
Jeonju Hanok Village **jeonjuhanongmaeul**
  전주 한옥마을
juice **juseu** 주스

K

Kakaotalk (SNS) **kakaotok** 카카오톡
key chain **yeolsoegori** 열쇠고리
Kimchi stew, a spicy stew made of kimchi,
onion, tofu, meat and kimchi juice
gimchijjigae 김치찌개
know **alda** 알다
Korean dry sauna **jjiljilbang** 찜질방
Korean food **hansik** 한식
Korean pop music *K-pop*
Korean traditional clothes **hanbok** 한복
Korean traditional clothes **hangugin** 한국인

L

laptop **noteubuk** 노트북
late (to be late) **neutda** 늦다
later **itta** 이따
later **najung** 나중
learn **baeuda** 배우다
leave behind **namgida** 남기다
leave, put **duda** 두다
left (direction) **oen** 왼
light **gabyeopda** 가볍다
like **joahada** 좋아하다
line **hoseon** 호선
listen **deutda** 듣다
little **jom** 좀 (short form for 조금 **jogeum**)
long time (long time no see) **oraenmanida**
오랜만이다
Lotte World **rotde woldeu** 롯데 월드
Lotte World Tower **rotdewoldeutawo**
롯데월드타워
luggage **suhamul** 수하물
lunch **jeomsim** 점심

M

magnet **jaseok** 자석
major **jeongong** 전공
makeup **hwajangpum** 화장품
manners **ye** 예
manners **yeui** 예의
market **sijang** 시장
marriage **gyeolhon** 결혼
marry (to get married) **gyeolhonhada**
결혼하다
mart **mateu** 마트
maybe **hoksi** 혹시
means **sudan** 수단
meet **mannada** 만나다
method **sudan** 수단
Mexico **meksiko** 멕시코
microwave (oven) **jeonjareinji** 전자레인지
mirror **geoul** 거울
Monday **woryoil** 월요일
month **dal** 달
morning **achim** 아침

most **jeil** 제일
mouth **ip** 입
movie **yeonghwa** 영화
movie theater **yeonghwagwan** 영화관
mug **meogeujan** 머그잔
music **eumak** 음악
must-eat place **matjip** 맛집
Myeong-dong **myeongdong** 명동

N

Naengmyeon **naengmyeon** 냉면
Namdaemun Market **namdaemunsijang**
남대문시장
name **ireum** 이름
Namsan Mountain **namsan** 남산
nap **natjam** 낮잠
national flag **gukgi** 국기
National Folk Museum of Korea
gungnimminsokbangmulgwan
국립민속박물관
National Museum of Korea
gungnipjungangbangmulgwan
국립중앙박물관
natural (to be natural) **dangyeonhada**
당연하다
NAVER (portal site) **neibeo** 네이버
neck **mok** 목
Netflix **netpeullikseu** 넷플릭스
New Zealand **nyujillaendeu** 뉴질랜드
next month **daeumdal** 다음달
next to **yeop** 옆
nice to meet (to be nice to meet) **bangapda**
반갑다
night **bam** 밤
no need **piryoeopda** 필요없다
nose **ko** 코
not be (to not be) (preceded by a verb) **ji anta**
-지 않다
not be (to not be) **anta** 않다
not be okay (to not be okay) **andoeda** 안되다
not exist **eopda** 없다
not know **moreuda** 모르다
not very **byeollo** 별로
notebook **noteu** 노트
now **jigeum** 지금

O

observatory **jeonmangdae** 전망대
ocean **bada** 바다
of course **dangyeonhada** 당연하다
okay (to be okay) **gwaenchanta** 괜찮다
old **oraedoeda** 오래되다
older brother of a male **hyeong** 형
older sister of a male **nuna** 누나
one-way trip **pyeondo** 편도
order food **jumunhada** 주문하다

order food **sikida** 시키다
organize (to organize) **jeongnihada** 정리하다
ornament **jangsikpum** 장식품

P

package **taekbae** 택배
paper money **jipye** 지폐
park **gongwon** 공원
parking **jucha** 주차
parking lot **juchajang** 주차장
particular **teukbyeolhada** 특별한
party **pati** 파티
passport **yeogwon** 여권
pasta **paseuta** 파스타
payment **gyeolje** 결제
payment **gyesan** 계산
peaceful **pyeongonhada** 평온하다
pencil **yeonpil** 연필
people counter **myeong** 명
perchance **hoksi** 혹시
performance **gongyeon** 공연
performance **yeongi** 연기
perfume **hyangsu** 향수
pharmacy **yakguk** 약국
phone number **jeonhwabeonho** 전화번호
pizza **pija** 피자
place **de** 데
porch **hyeongwan** 현관
pork belly **samgyeopsal** 삼겹살
post office **ucheguk** 우체국
postcard **yeopseo** 엽서
pretty (to be pretty) **yeppeuda** 예쁘다
price **gagyeok** 가격
promise **yaksok** 약속
purchase **gumae** 구매
quick (to be quick) **ppareuda** 빠르다

R

rainy season **jangma** 장마
rap artist **raepeo** 래퍼
rapper **raepeo** 래퍼
read **ikda** 읽다
really **jinjja** 진짜
receipt **yeongsujeung** 영수증
refrigerator **naengjanggo** 냉장고
regard **daehada** 대하다
remain **namda** 남다
reservation **yeyak** 예약
resort **rijoteu** 리조트
respect **jongyeong** 존경
rest **swida** 쉬다
restaurant specializing in meat **gogitjip** 고기집
restroom **hwajangsil** 화장실
rice **bap** 밥
rice ball **jumeokbap** 주먹밥

rice cake **tteok** 떡
ride (a car, train, or bike) **tada** 타다
ride (amusement park) **nori gigu** 놀이 기구
right (direction) **oreun** 오른
right (to be right) (agreeing with another's opinion) **matda** 맞다
rinse **rinseu** 린스
roller coaster **rolleokoseuteo** 롤러코스터
room **bang** 방
roommate **rummeiteu** 룸메이트
round trip **wangbok** 왕복
Russia **reosia** 러시아

S

sandwich **saendeuwichi** 샌드위치
Saturday **toyoil** 토요일
school **hakgyo** 학교
season **gyejeol** 계절
seaweed soup **miyeokguk** 미역국
see **boda** 보다
senior **seonbae** 선배
Seoul **seoul** 서울
Seoul Arts Center **yesuruijeondang** 예술의 전당
Seoul Station **seoul-yeok** 서울역
shampoo **syampu** 샴푸
ship **bae** 배
shoe closet **sinbaljang** 신발장
shoes **sinbal** 신발
shoulder **eokkae** 어깨
show **boyeojuda** 보여주다
siblings **hyeongje** 형제
sick (to be sick) **apeuda** 아프다
sightsee **gugyeonghada** 구경하다
sightseeing **gugyeong** 구경
SIM card **yusimchip** 유심칩
singer **gasu** 가수
sleep (honorific) **jumusida** 주무시다
sleep **jada** 자다
snack **gwaja** 과자
so **geuraeseo** 그래서
sofa **sopa** 소파
soft tofu stew **sundubujjigae** 순두부찌개
sometimes **gakkeum** 가끔
South Korea **hanguk** 한국
souvenir **ginyeompum** 기념품
Spain **seupein** 스페인
spend (time) **jinaeda** 지내다
spicy (to be spicy) **maepda** 맵다
spoon **sutgarak** 숟가락
spring **bom** 봄
station **jeongnyujang** 정류장
station platform **seunggangjang** 승강장
straight **baro** 바로
straight (direction) **jikjin** 직진
straining (to be straining) **himdeulda** 힘들다

streaming service **seuteuriming seobiseu** 스트리밍 서비스
study **gongbuhada** 공부하다
subway (underground) **jihacheol** 지하철
subway **jeoncheol** 전철
subway line **hoseon** 호선
subway station **yeok** 역
subway stop **jeonggeojang** 정거장
summer **yeoreum** 여름
Sunday **iryoil** 일요일
sunny **makda** 맑다
Sweden **seuweden** 스웨덴
swimming pool **suyeongjang** 수영장

T

take a class **sueobeul deutda** 수업을 듣다
take a walk **sanchaekada** 산책하다
take off **beotda** 벗다
taxi **taeksi** 택시
television **tellebijeon** 텔레비전
thankful **gamsahada** 감사하다
thanks to **deokbune** 덕분에
that (close to listener) **geogi(geu)** 거기(그)
that (not close to either the listener or speaker) **jeogi(jeo)** 저기(저)
the best **choego** 최고
the Blue House **cheongwadae** 청와대
the seat number **jwaseokbeonho** 좌석번호
the United Kingdom **yeongguk** 영국
the West **seoyang** 서양
think **seanggakada** 생각하다
this (close to speaker) **yeogi(i)** 여기(이)
Thursday **mogyoil** 목요일
ticket **tiket** 티켓
ticket office **maepyoso** 매표소
time **sigan** 시간
time **ttae** 때
time difference **sicha** 시차
time table **siganpyo** 시간표
tired (to be tired) **pigonhada** 피곤하다
today **oneul** 오늘
together **gachi** 같이
tomorrow **naeil** 내일
toothbrush **chitsol** 칫솔
toothpaste **chiyak** 치약
traffic lights **sinhodeung** 신호등
train **gicha** 기차
train destination **haeng** -행
train station **gichayeok** 기차역
train ticket **gichapyo** 기차표
transfer **garatada** 갈아타다
transfer **hwanseunghada** 환승하다

transportation **gyotong** 교통
transportation card **gyotongkadeu** 교통카드
travel **yeohaeng** 여행
Tuesday **hwayoil** 화요일

U

Ulsan **ulsan** 울산
umbrella **usan** 우산
under-floor heating system **ondol** 온돌
underground **jihacheung** 지하층
up to a certain point **kkaji** 까지
use **iyonghada** 이용하다
use **sayonghada** 사용하다
use **sseuda** 쓰다
utilize **iyonghada** 이용하다

V

vacant **bin (cha)** 빈 (차)
vacation **hyuga** 휴가
vicinity **geuncheo** 근처
visa **bija** 비자
visit **bangmunhada** 방문하다

W

walk **sanchaek** 산책
warm (to be warm) **ttatteutada** 따뜻하다
washing machine **setakgi** 세탁기
watch **boda** 보다
weather **nalssi** 날씨
Wednesday **suyoil** 수요일
weekend **jumal** 주말
welcome **eoseooseyo** 어서오세요
what **mwo** 뭐
wheat noodles **milmyeon** 밀면
where **eodi** 어디
which **eoneu** 어느
window **changmun** 창문
winter **gyeoul** 겨울
work **il** 일
worldwide **segyejeok** 세계적
worry **geokjeonghada** 걱정하다
wow **uwa** 우와
wow **wa** 와

Y

yesterday **eoje** 어제
you're welcome **anida** 아니다 (basic meaning is "no.")
younger brother **namdongsaeng** 남동생
younger sibling **dongsaeng** 동생
younger sister **yeodongsaeng** 여동생

Photo Credits

The following photos used in this book are from Shutterstock:

Cover image © Portrait Image Asia and Filip Bjorkman
Page 4 © chai photographer
Page 41 © kikujungboy CC
Page 45 © mentatdgt
Page 49 © siro46
Page 60 © Monkey Business Images
Page 67 © Jimmy Yan
Page71 © imtmphoto
Page 79 © imtmphoto
Page 86 © PANDECH
Page 113 © Silvia Elizabeth Pangaro
Page 127 © Foto by KKK
Page 170 © shin sang eun

and one from Dreamstime:

Page 139 © Jamesbox

To Access the Online Audio Recordings and Flashcards:

1. Check to be sure you have an internet connection.
2. Type the URL below into your web browser.
   https://www.tuttlepublishing.com/learning-korean

For support, you can email us at info@tuttlepublishing.com.